White-Knuckled Mothering

– GRASPING ONTO BIBLICAL TRUTH THROUGH THE LITTLE YEARS –

by Hannah Unger

White-Knuckled Mothering: Grasping onto Biblical Truth through the Little Years

First Edition, Month 2019

Publisher

Lincoln, Nebraska

Editing: Shayla Raquel, ShaylaRaquel.com

Cover Design: Deb Lee Toth, DebLeeToth.myportfolio.com

Interior Formatting: Rogena Mitchell-Jones, RogenaMitchell.com

ISBN 978-0-578-48005-3

To Lincoln, Braddock, Mack, and Bishop: By being your mom, I've seen and felt the kindness and goodness of my Heavenly Father.

Thank you for the honor, my sons.

CONTENTS

INTRODUCTION

"A mother is a chalice, the vessel without which no human being has ever been born. She is created to be a life-bearer, cooperating with her husband and with God in the making of a child. What a solemn responsibility. What an unspeakable privilege—a vessel divinely prepared for the Master's use."

—Elisabeth Elliot, The Shaping of a Christian Family

Mothering small children is one of the hardest, most challenging, exhausting things I've ever willingly attempted in life. Most times, you are either mind-numbingly tired or . . . wait . . . there is no "or"—you are always tired. You've accepted the hard truth that this sort of living is going to be your reality for the next handful of years.

I am by no means an expert in the field of mothering small children. I don't think I have this brand-new outlook on how to be a godly mother, but I do have an honest outlook on what the Lord has taught me in my first handful of years of being a mom.

As moms, it's easy and natural to be passionate about our children. They are our world, after all. They are our constant companions needing our undivided attention. But why are these little people whom we love so much so exhausting? Why is it that one minute, we feel like we've got this mothering thing down, and the next minute, we feel like we're drowning because we forgot to put lifejackets on everyone—ourselves included? If you've ever felt that way, then I wrote this book for you.

These are the stories I'd probably share with you over a cup of strong coffee, sitting outside on my backyard patio or sitting on my well-worn, used couch with our kids running amuck. I'd recall these stories to encourage you to keep going, keep trying, keep seeking, keep praying, and keep growing. I'd tell you these things, and then I'd offer you the chance to go take a nap while I watch your kids, because what mom doesn't need a nap?

But this book isn't just for mothers. It's for moms who have a relationship with the Lord, who are daily reading the Bible and spending time in prayer, and who are in fellowship with a local church. Maybe you're a Christian mom, but you're not doing those things (but you know you should). By the end of this book, you'll feel encouraged in your work as a mother. You'll be reminded that what God has called you to do as a mother is worthy and honorable. I hope you will view all of these hours we are logging in the middle of the night feeding babies and taking care of crying toddlers as seen. You'll be reminded you are not alone, not even close.

I want to encourage you with knowing that a messy life doesn't always mean an unfruitful one (and I'm not talking about the cleanliness of your home).

I don't want to give a false picture of my life or over glorify my sons and the things they've learned, but I do want to glorify what my Heavenly Father has done for us and what He has shown me and taught me.

Sometimes, I feel so much like Paul in the Bible when he says in I Timothy 1:15 (NIV), "Christ Jesus came into the world to save sinners of whom I am the worst," because I have so many loud flaws and very apparent sins that like to live proudly. But aren't we fully aware of our flaws and weaknesses? Let's not just be aware, but let's be growing and changing. Think about when you brought your first baby home or maybe you're on your first baby and thinking (or thought), *I can't be doing this right. It doesn't feel like I'm doing this the right way*. You are not some anomaly. Don't we want to be growing and changing and not the same mother we were when we brought that first baby home? We want to be able to look back and see our Heavenly Father's fingerprints all over our lives. We want to see evidence of change and not just survival.

I'm going to share some things I learned in those "first baby" years. My hope is that it resonates and encourages you not to just settle for survival mode but also to encourage you to see real, fought-for, strived-for growth.

As I said, I don't believe I have a brand-new outlook on godly mothering or a fresh approach that no one has ever thought about, but I do know what I know. I have what God has taught me through my first eight years of mothering, such as:

- mothering is God's specifically designed curriculum to grow you;
- there is purpose to be found in the mundane; and
- we must view these critical years through eyes of faith.

I want to encourage you in your day-to-day of "laying down your life for the least of these" (Matthew 25:40, NIV, paraphrasing).

As moms, with the same hopes and dreams for our kids, isn't that a common thing we long for—an encouragement, a reassuring "you're not alone" statement, a little push to finish the day strong and right in the middle of His will for your life? If that's your expectation with these words, please continue reading, because that's my hope: that these words could encourage you to bear-hug this calling of ours, of godly motherhood.

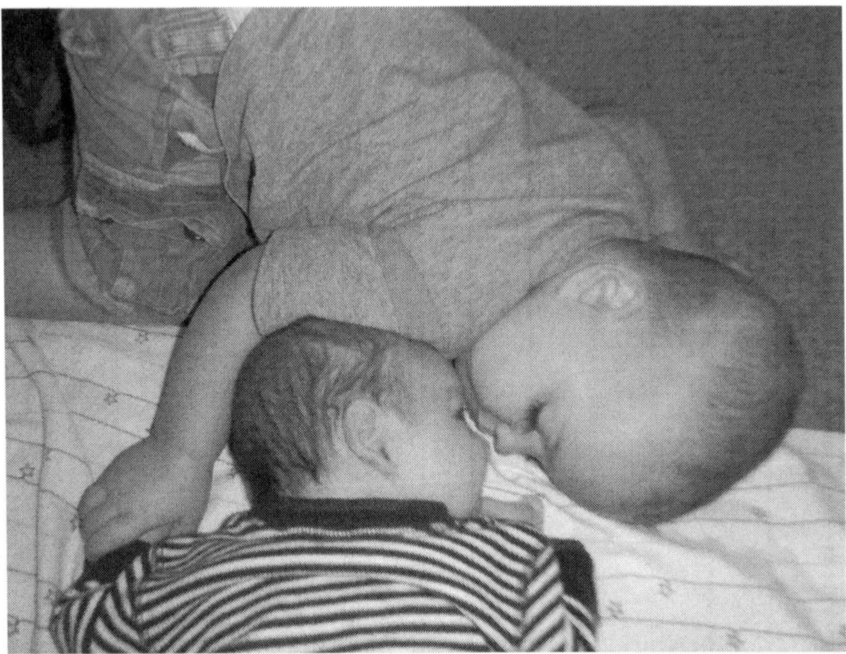

1

AUTHORITY: IS IT REALLY NECESSARY?

"It is a great mistake to think they should understand all they learn! For God has ordered that in youth the memory should act vigorously, independent of the understanding—whereas a man cannot usually recollect a thing unless he understands it."

—Thomas Arnold

Authority. Who possesses it in your home? Who's in charge—like, *really* in charge? If there's a lot of what I like to call "suggestive parenting," then you probably already know the answer to this question.

When you think of an authority figure, do you imagine any of these?

- a dictator of the home
- someone always barking out orders
- someone demanding to be in charge and respected
- someone ruling the roost with an iron fist, demanding obedience

If you see authority as any of those above, then you need to redefine its meaning. When I ask, "Who possesses the authority in your home?" I'm really asking, "Who obeys whom? Who is instructing whom with what's best for their life? Is it you, the parent, or is it your children?"

This question may make you uncomfortable while reflecting on your daily life, but let me share with you a story about when my husband and I faced this very question.

It was back when we had one child, and the second was quickly approaching his arrival. Our two oldest boys are fifteen months apart, so clearly, we needed the only crib in the house. We decided it was time to transition our oldest to a "big boy bed." My husband and I were way too logical (or maybe cheap), because the idea of buying a second crib was out of the question.

"Why buy a second one with a perfectly good one in the house?" we said. "We'll just put Linc, our oldest, in a big bed."

So, my husband Shane gets the bed set up, lays our fifteen-month-old down for bedtime, turns off the light, closes the door, and comes downstairs. Little did we know that night we willfully and ignorantly began a battle that raged for over a year.

He'd sneak toys into his bed, turn on the light, walk out, sneak downstairs, and peer at us from behind corners. Every night, we hoped that by doing nothing, something was going to change. Ridiculous, right? We'd just get situated on the couch downstairs, ice cream out of the freezer, beer opened, a show started, and we'd see little pudgy feet trotting down the stairs.

So what were we to do now?

We didn't call it quits and buy another crib and put him back in one. We didn't shrug and say, "Guess he's just not ready." We may have ignorantly led our son into this battle, but now we—the authority of this little guy, the people who call the shots—were now called to *finish* the battle and win.

Here we were faced with a choice. Did we begin to establish our authority over our son, or did we allow him to establish his will over *us*? Realizing we were his parents didn't mean he was going to start automatically obeying us. In a parent-child relationship, there are usually two wills. We either relent to the willpower of our children, or we believe that we know what's best and show them how to obey us.

BATTLE OF THE WILLS

I love reading books from the preachers of old. They write with conviction and boldness that I think our culture can find wanting. One of my favorites is J. C. Ryle. He wrote a little book (that I highly recommend) called *The Duties of Parents*. Here's a quote from him:

> "Deal wisely with your child, you must not leave him to the guidance of his own will. Think for him, judge for him, act for him, just as you would for one weak and blind; but for pity's sake, give him not up to his own wayward tastes and inclinations. It must not be his likings and wishes that are consulted. He knows not yet what is good for his mind and soul, any more than what is good for his body. Self-will is almost the first thing that appears in a child's mind; and it must be your first step to resist it.[1]

So our fifteen-month-old was still fighting us tooth and nail, not wanting to accept our authority in his little life. There were two agendas those nights and two wills that were raging against each other. We wanted him to sleep where and when we told him to, and he wanted his own way and to be able to play whenever he wanted. He didn't want to be told what to do.

We decided to engage. Every night, my husband or I would sit outside his door after we laid him down and turned off the light. We were ready to discipline the moment he chose to disobey us. The second we heard those little feet hit the ground, we went in, disciplined him, hugged him, tucked him back into bed, and reminded him, "Stay in bed, Linc, and go to sleep."

Every single night, he disobeyed. He wasn't yet convinced we were in charge, and he was determined to win. Any given evening, you'd find my husband or I sitting there on the ground outside his door, book in hand or with a laptop working. Sometimes, we would be sitting there just catching up on our day, whispering in the hallway. So many times, we would question each other.

"Is there something we're missing here? What are we doing wrong? Why isn't spanking working? Would a toddler bed work better? A night-light? The perfect sound machine?"

Or maybe, just maybe, the Lord had orchestrated a circumstance for us (the parents) to establish authority over our toddler, and He was asking us to persevere. What if we had forfeited that circumstance? Isn't the Lord faithful enough to then orchestrate another circumstance further down the road in our child's life for us to win? Doesn't He love our kids so much that He's going to keep asking us to win *with* them? And then, if we never win, does that mean we raised our children without any sense of what authority is? Doesn't that make sense? That we are the first people our children are supposed to learn how to obey? And I say "learn" because it doesn't come naturally. In fact, in my limited experience, most of the time, they fight it with all their might. Just because our little people may resist and fight against our authority doesn't mean we give in and let them have their way. Maybe it would help encourage us on those long days and nights of teaching our children to obey those in charge to remember that God has very specifically given us this task as parents.

In Genesis 18:19 (NIV), God says about Abraham, "For I have

chosen him, so that he will direct his children and his household after him to keep the way of the Lord by doing what is right and just."

Do you believe that's true of you also, that God has chosen you specifically to be the parent of your child and He's given you a specific job? That job is to direct your children, not be directed by them. It's for you to show them what's right, and not just the other way around. Leading and directing require authority. Another quote from the great J. C. Ryle:

> To my eyes, a parent always yielding, and a child always having its own way, are a most painful sight; painful, because I see God's appointed order of things inverted and turned upside down, painful, because I feel sure the consequence to that child's character in the end will be self-will, pride, and self-conceit. You must not wonder that men refuse to obey their Father which is in heaven, if you allow them, when children, to disobey their father who is on earth.[2]

We need to learn to engage because, for most of us, that doesn't come naturally. As the people who are with them most hours of every day, if we aren't teaching our kids to obey us and to do what we ask of them, why do we think they're going to grow up and obey God?

KEEP AT IT

A couple of months in, my husband and I realized the severity of this battle and what the Lord was asking of us. We stood our ground, shared the load of discipline at night, encouraged each other, and fervently prayed we'd win this battle soon. Month after month passed. It felt like absolutely nothing was accomplished. We were no closer to victory than we were the first night this started. Every night that passed seemed like the Lord was answering our prayers with a "keep at it."

One night, my husband came downstairs after what seemed like a shorter time than the night before. Sure enough, it was. It was only a two-hour battle that night. Then, more time passed, and one night, he came downstairs after just one hour. *Is this working?* I thought.

After more time, more nights, more weeks, more months of being faithful and consistent, after the one-year mark of the beginning of our battle, he stayed in bed. He stayed in bed the next night and the following nights. We won. We showed our little man that Mom and Dad were in charge—and we meant to stay there. Our hope was that one day, when we, his parents, were no longer in charge of him, the authority would transfer from us to God smoothly because we taught him how to obey authority.

"God appointed parental rule in the family as the symbol of His own authority." —Andrew Murray

We still had nights every so often when we had to remind Linc, "No, it's not okay to get out of bed." But guess what? Our eight-year-old now goes to bed when we ask him to. And he has been obedient in this area for many years now. And as we have added brothers to his room, he's shown them when they transition to a big boy bed how to *stay* in bed at night.

Right now, we have four boys in bunk beds sharing one room, and bedtime is peaceful. Sure, we have to remind them sometimes that there's no talking at bedtime and they have to stay in bed after lights out. I firmly believe that if we had not won with our oldest, bedtime would look very differently today. I know for sure all four boys sharing a room wouldn't have been possible. That's why it's so important to engage with the battles the Lord puts in front of you, because you don't know how He wants to use them in the future.

And get this: our eight-year-old still loves us. That yearlong battle didn't hinder our relationship with him, but I know it's because we weren't demanding our authority over him. We were slowly, gently showing him this is how things are, and that it's a good thing, a safe thing for him.

"The entrance of divine truth into the mind and heart, the formation of habits and the training of character—these are not attained by sudden and isolated efforts, but by regular and unceasing repetition." —Andrew Murray

If we're drill sergeants who demand obedience, we'll close their hearts toward us and the authority we're trying to establish. We need to embrace the season the Lord has us in with our child and not fight the length of the season He has ordained.

"What kind of picture are your children getting of God's authority by the way you exercise yours? Establishing authority early in little things is doing gospel work." —Paul David Tripp

"Anger and harshness may frighten, but they will not persuade the child that you are right; and if he sees you often out of temper, you will soon cease to have his respect." — J. C. Ryle

Those quotes are so hard for me to read because those very things—anger, harshness, sternness, and severity of manner—are my natural tendencies. I need to fight hard against letting these things be a part of my parenting. Instead, I need what J. C. Ryle suggests:

> “ Love should be the silver thread that runs through all your conduct. Kindness, gentleness, long-suffering,

> forbearance, patience, sympathy, a willingness to enter into childish troubles, a readiness to take part in childish joys—these are the cords by which a child may be led most easily—these are the clues you must follow if you would find the way to his heart.[3]

Establishing authority this way also gains access to children's hearts, which is vital if we plan on teaching them anything in life. Our eight-year-old is very secure because he knows Mom and Dad are in charge and he can trust us. He's completely confident in his trust in us, his parents. He knows he's not in charge and, honestly, he takes comfort in that.

What small child wants the burden of being in charge? They may want their way, but they want to know they're being looked out for. They may be fighting tooth and nail at your establishing authority over them, but if you succeed in doing it the way God has instructed you, I guarantee the peace in your home will increase by leaps and bounds. But it takes work and effort on your part to get there.

At the beginning of this chapter, I mentioned "suggestive parenting," which is a term I came up with all on my own. You're welcome. Suggestive parenting is when parents avoid being the authoritative role in their children's lives because it causes friction. Instead, they resort to *suggesting* things as opposed to telling or instructing the child.

For instance, a suggestive parent says:

- "Hey, should we go take a nap?"
- "Do you think we should turn off the iPad?"
- "Are you ready to eat lunch yet?"
- "Is it time to go home from the park now?"

Is there more suggesting going on in your home as opposed to directing and instructing? And when I say "instructing," I mean simply telling your child that it's naptime/bedtime/mealtime/time to go and expect them to obey. Remember, not like a dictator, but in a loving, gentle "I know what's best for you" kind of way. Are you able to ask things of your toddlers (yes, toddlers), knowing they'll obey? It *is* possible for a toddler who can't yet speak to obey you.

Or are you walking on eggshells hoping not to rock the boat and cause a temper tantrum in the grocery store? In fact, do you avoid asking them to do things or telling them no because you know screaming and outbursts will follow? If any of this sounds familiar, then maybe you need to ask yourself if you have established authority in your children's lives.

Are we willing to engage and establish the authority God has given us to have over our little people? We can win authority *and* their hearts simultaneously. Remember, everything your Heavenly Father is asking of you as a parent is to win your children, and it is usually rooted in an act of obedience to your Savior. Do you believe that? That something as seemingly small as winning in bedtime or mealtime could have eternal effects? I believe it, and I'm treating it as eternal work.

ACTION TIPS:

- Take an honest evaluation of your home. Ask yourself the sometimes-hard questions: "Who is in charge between my kids and me?" or "Have I established authority in my child's life in a God-honoring way?"
- If the answer is no, then start asking God what areas in your child's life you should begin addressing first.
- Begin obeying your Heavenly Father by asking your child to obey you. Immediately.

2

BATTLING BETWEEN OUR EARS

"If God does not save men by truth,
He certainly will not save them by lies."

—Charles Spurgeon

I'd like to talk about an age-old struggle for women. Women have battled with this for centuries and centuries, and with it, joy and confidence have been robbed. Contentment all tainted because of this. Insecurities, fears, and doubt are all side effects of this battle. You may already have in mind what I'm talking about.

If you guessed *comparison,* you guessed right. Oh, how Satan loves to blind us women from our work for the day. How he loves to steal our joy right out from underneath us with comparison. He's good at it too. He knows how to distract us, discourage us, and speak lies to us. And he does it all right between our ears and our minds, the unseen battleground. It's the battleground that's only between you and God or between you and the great Deceiver.

In today's day and age, one of the easiest avenues of ushering in this age-old struggle with comparing is social media (unless you're one of the few who have stayed away from social media's claws). If you're one of the majority like me who's on social media and mostly enjoys it, then you and I have to be aware of the kinds of struggles it can bring for the Christian woman.

While on Instagram, I can have a view of people's lives as often as they want me to. In real life, I see into people's lives only when I'm with them in the flesh. I love Instagram—don't get me wrong! I'm one of those moms who posts way too much about her kids, and I use plenty of cheesy hashtags. But the danger of this platform for women is the battle in our minds it creates.

How many of you were having a perfectly fine day, and then you happen to see a picture on your favorite social media network that immediately causes a flood of emotions? I know I can't be the only woman this has happened to. Am I the only one who, at times, is giving more attention to my Instagram feed than to my kids when they try to explain their latest LEGO creation?

Am I the only one who picks up my phone more than my toddler? You're on Instagram, and you see a group of your friends got together the other night, and right away, you're hurt. You think, *Why wasn't I invited? Is someone mad at me? I've been an awful friend lately, so that must be why.* All of these feelings and lies rush in and settle very cozily in your thoughts.

And they intend to stay awhile.

Comparison can show up in so many different forms. You see a video or picture of a friend's kid who's the same age as one of your kids, and they're doing something really cool (like riding a bike for the first time). You immediately start thinking, *My kid doesn't ride his bike yet; I've never even practiced with him.* Suddenly, guilt rushes in. You see your friend just bought your dream home with a wrap-around porch out in the country with shiplap on every interior wall. And instead of being so happy for her, you're filled with envy and discontentment.

The list goes on. Your kids versus other kids. Your friend who has a garden and only eats organically. Your friend who keeps telling you about a workout regimen at home. Will you ever really be fit? You see a family having devotions together, and instead of being so encouraged to do the same, you're filled with lies and feelings that are not from above.

"Comparison is the thief of joy." —Theodore Roosevelt

Oy, Teddy knew what was up when he said that. It's true, and it's annoying. When we see those things on social media or have a conversation in real life with somebody, and we walk away from that person believing that we are failing as a mom and a friend and a human, what can we do? We should engage in these battles of lies that plague us.

And what's the surest way to defeat a lie? With the truth from above and through prayer. Crying out to the Lord with what you're feeling. He already knows, but He wants you to offer it up to Him and give it over to His capable hands. He has bucket loads of truth He could give us if only we'd ask for them. If only we would research the Word for His truth to battle the areas we face on the regular.

I remember I used to have this mentality that I was subject to whatever thoughts disguised as lies would enter my head. Just live with it until it goes away. But I would find that sometimes these feelings were plaguing me for days, which turned into a week, and then I just spent the whole week feeling things, carrying things that the Lord never wanted me to carry in the first place but that He also wanted to take off my heart so I could focus on my children, my husband, and my home wholeheartedly. Instead of addressing these unhealthy feelings, I started swirling down self-centered, woeful thinking. Clearly, it was *not* healthy. I know this isn't where every woman ends up with her thinking, but this is where I would end up.

Our tendencies and weaknesses don't have to be our lifelong

companions. God wants to help us overcome them. He wants to help us see victory, but it ultimately starts with us deciding to engage. I've also noticed that growth in this area isn't always instant. It takes practice over and over and over again. It takes us recognizing that we're believing or listening to a lie, or we're comparing ourselves to others. It takes the recognition to know where these lies originate. Is it coming from above or below? Who wants you to believe what you hear in your head?

William Backus said in his book *Telling Yourself the Truth*, "The misbeliefs/lies we tell ourselves are directly from the pit of hell. They are hand engraved and delivered by the devil himself." Think about that! Those lies you're struggling with didn't magically appear out of thin air. No, they were very specifically designed for your personality and hand-delivered right between your ears by someone who wants to destroy you. Imagine with me that Satan is sitting in front of you with a bowl in hand. He has mixed up a steaming, rancid bowl of mushy lies that he intends to feed you. He's put this mush in a pretty bowl to hopefully trick you into thinking that it will actually taste good. So here he sits in front of you very patiently and consistently spoon-feeding you the lies he has mixed up just for you.

All the while, your Heavenly Father is standing by watching this whole situation play out. In His hands, He also offers you something to eat. What He's offering is a beautiful, juicy steak full of truth. He knows what He offers is good for you. He knows it tastes delicious, but He also doesn't force you to choose His steak dinner. He gives you free will to choose whatever you want to stay in your mind. He isn't going to force you to believe His truth and how He feels about you. You need to choose to slap that spoon out of Satan's hand and ask for the plate of truth that your Heavenly Father always has hot and ready to serve.

Once you recognize the lie, then it's on to combat it. I'll tell you this: combating these feelings is not accomplished through positive thinking. It is intentionally praying and meditating on things above. It's training your mind to stop going down that path of thinking over and over again. It's crying out to the Lord for His help when you recognize that your mind is drifting from things above. Over and over and over again.

"Pessimists are usually right and optimists are usually wrong, but all the great changes have been accomplished by optimists."
—Thomas L. Friedman

How we think matters. How we think about ourselves, our children, our husbands, our calling in life, and those around us. How we think about these areas will be followed by action at some point. I decided I needed to memorize some verses to help me in this area. I needed something in my arsenal, something I had on hand that I was able to draw from—quickly. I started with Philippians 4:8 (NIV):

Finally, brothers and sisters, whatever is true, whatever is noble, whatever is right, whatever is pure, whatever is lovely, whatever is admirable—if anything is excellent or praiseworthy—think about such things.

That verse right there became my checklist.

- Is this true and noble?
- Is it pure and lovely?
- Is it admirable, excellent, and praiseworthy?

If it didn't fall into those categories, I needed to stop. But how? Well, let me share a couple examples of how I've learned to stop believing these lies.

One of my sons is a thinker and a feeler. Most of his battles seem to happen right in that beautiful brain of his. He's more emotional than his brothers and he feels things strongly. I remember one rough week in particular. My son had been corrected and disciplined quite a bit. Once again, he and I found ourselves back in my bedroom, sitting on my bed talking about his wrong behavior toward his brother. I disciplined him and gave him a hug, and we were supposed to be good again. He was still very clearly upset; he was crying very hard and still very emotional. I asked him why he was still upset, to which he said, "I'm your worst kid. I get disciplined the most. I'm just the worst." Talk about a sucker punch to the gut for this mom!

Here was my five-year-old son hearing and believing a lie from the pit of hell. How dare Satan spoon-feed his lies to him. So here I was seeing and hearing my son who was feeling something so strongly that he believed it was true. Now I had to step in and help preach truth to my son's head and heart. I assured him I loved him so much, and that God loved him. I told him his behavior is never going to change my love for him, and that I am pleased with him. Then I had him repeat it back to me. I had him verbally speak truth to his own little heart and mind.

That was such a perfect picture of what we as Christian women need to be doing sometimes on an hourly basis throughout our day. We need to identify that lie that feels so real and call it what it is: a lie. Then we need to replace it with truth from our Heavenly Father and we need to fight to keep that truth there.

I can think of another instance that keeps reiterating the importance of replacing lies and unhealthy thinking patterns with truth. Sometimes at night, one of my boys will come into our room and tell us he had a bad dream. So, we pray with him, remind him of scriptures like, "When I am afraid, I will put my trust in You," and then we tell them to start thinking of something else. We help give them ideas like, "Think about the fun day we are going to have tomorrow" or "Think about going to Nana and Papa's at Christmastime when all your cousins are there and how much fun we have." We try to help them start thinking about something different and positive. Scripture accompanied by intentionally redirected thoughts is effective. Isn't that what the verse in Philippians is talking about when it says to "think on these things"? Even when it's hard to focus and think on things above, do it! Turn your mind and your thoughts to truth—the truth that's found in our Creator's love letter to us.

Isn't this the same concept with us women? If we cry out to the Lord for help and have verses of truth on hand to speak to our hearts, then we can distract our minds from the thoughts we don't want there. Speaking truth to your heart is never in vain. We can't let words someone wrote on our social media feed occupy our thoughts more than what we read in the Bible and heard the Lord say to us that morning. Maybe it's time to put down our phones and pick up our Bibles more. Maybe it's time to quiet down the ever-present noise of outside voices so we can hear our Heavenly Father's voice. It's typically quieter and gentler than all the other voices.

The distractions we willingly place in front of our eyes on an hourly basis are stealing us away from our work.

Kathleen Nelson once said, "Motherhood is urgent work." I agree completely and wholeheartedly. Do you? Do we treat it as such? Do we realize how quickly these years pass?

I don't have these kids in my home for very long. How can I allow myself to be mentally out of the game on an hourly basis?

And I am constantly allowing these lies to have a megaphone into my mind and heart. Is this one of the struggles that the modern Christian woman can face? I think so. For those of us who do struggle with accepting lies as truth, we need to get serious about winning. Otherwise, I'm afraid we could lose right in the middle of our homes on the battleground between our ears.

ACTION TIPS:

- Identify the lies you are hearing in your life. Make a list if it helps.
- Recognize the lies for what they are. *Lies.*
- Search in Scripture truths to combat the lies you're hearing/entertaining/believing. Add those verses to your list.
- Claim those truths and knock that spoon of lies out of Satan's hand and live in the truth that is offered to you.

3

FLOWERS ARE HARD TO GROW

"You are entitled to your own opinion, but you are not entitled to your own truth"

—RC Sproul

One of the hardest things I had to learn as a Christian mom was what my husband and I believed about disciplining our children. What kind of household were we going to be? Pro-spanking? Pro-timeouts? Pro "ignore their behavior and hope they magically learn what they should be doing"?

I was raised in a Christian household by two parents who loved the Lord and did their very best at raising seven kids according to biblical standards. There was no question in our minds that my mom and dad loved us. Just like there was no question in our minds that if we didn't obey them, we would get a spanking for our disobedience. We knew Mom and Dad spanked us when we did wrong because the Bible told parents to do so: "No discipline seems pleasant at the time, but painful. Later on, however, it produces a harvest of righteousness and peace for those who have been trained by it" (Hebrews 12:11, NIV). We didn't question it because that's what we knew. Mom and Dad did a great job at raising us in a peaceful, loving environment. We still had our struggles and hardships, but again, no one ever doubted that they were loved.

Fast-forward to my first son being born. Yay, we're parents! But then suddenly, he's a very disobedient toddler, and my husband and I are looking at each other thinking, *Should we do something about this?* Now, my husband was never disciplined or spanked (at least that he can recall), so he didn't have any idea what it would be like to discipline our chubby little toddler. We both very clearly saw this sin in him, which we knew needed to be addressed. So, we felt a bit lost and not entirely sure where to begin. Before I go on, let me share this metaphor with you.

One day, a package arrives on your doorstep. Inside it is a whole different array of seeds. Flower seeds! Also inside are a book and a note. The note says:

> *Here are my flower seeds! I have grand plans for these flowers. I need you to grow them for me, and when they are mature and ready to be used, I will come for them. All questions you may have regarding the growing of these flowers are in the* Flower Growing Manual *I sent along for you to read. Everything you need to know is in that manual. Happy growing.*
>
> — LOVE, GOD

How exciting and terrifying! It's terrifying because you don't have any idea how to grow flowers, and you have never grown plants in your life. Doubt, fears, and anxiety all creep in instantly. But wait, you remember the manual. Okay, you can do this. All of your questions can be answered in the manual. So, on day one, you read in the manual about planting these seeds. You read about what kind of soil you need, how much sun these kinds of flowers need, and how often you're going to need to water them. Then, you get to planting, feeling a bit more confident because you're just doing what the book says to do.

A couple months into your growing season, things seem to be going well. You see little green sprouts popping up from the ground —and they're growing! It's working! But then one morning, you go outside to check your garden and notice a funky-looking spot on your flowers. In fact, these spots seem to be spreading on the leaves. In alarm, you rush inside, grab the manual, and start searching for what you should do about this seeming disease. As you read, you learn that these flowers are prone to disease. But not to fret—there's a solution.

The more you read, the more uncomfortable you get with what the book is telling you to do to your precious flowers. It's saying you need to clip away the infected parts of the leaves. Cut the leaves? That doesn't seem right! Isn't that actually hurting the plants more? Plus, it's saying to mix up a solution of water and minerals, and you're supposed to spray your flowers at least three times a day. Three times a day? That's highly inconvenient. How are you supposed to maintain a normal life if you're constantly taking care of these flowers and their disease?

You decide there must be other methods to treat this disease. So, you start researching other options. Maybe something a little bit more modern or up-to-date with the times. Surely there can be a less drastic action. In fact, you start to question when this manual was published. Maybe it's outdated and not relevant as another material is nowadays. The manual eventually gets pushed to the back of the dresser, where it's forgotten and starts collecting dust. You can figure this out, right? You don't need that manual!

You forget these seeds were given to you for a reason by a specific person. You forget that the Lord wants to use them for something grand, and He intended that you raise these flowers according to His manual that He wrote and sent to you. But because we are uncomfortable with "the hows" on dealing with diseases, we disregard His method altogether and resort to whatever feels comfortable and easy for us.

This metaphor is obviously referring to the seeds as our kids and the manual as the Bible. How often do we dismiss things from the Bible written directly to us as parents because it just doesn't sit right with us?

All of our kids have the same disease in them as we do: sin. And God tells us how to address the sin in our children. The book of Proverbs is chock-full of verses specifically addressing parenting methods. But as Christian parents, how often do we forget to look to the Word for guidance on how to raise these God-given kids? Instead, we look to the world's methods and how they're telling us it should or shouldn't be done. Maybe we have looked to the Word, and even though we know what it says, we choose not to obey it.

It's very clear. Annoyingly clear at times. But it's up to us to believe that the Lord's methods are right, and our own methods, tendencies, or fears in this area are not.

The more my husband and I prayed about this and talked with other families who were ahead of us with raising godly families and what they did, and the more we searched the Word for guidance, we couldn't ignore the book of Proverbs. It's almost like God knew Christian parents' fears and tendencies not to obey Him in this area. He talks about it constantly, so we can't ignore it. Here are just a few verses we couldn't keep ignoring:

Proverbs 13:24 (KJ2000) — "He who spares his rod hates his son, but he who loves him chastens him early."

Proverbs 22:15 (NASB) — "Foolishness is bound up in the heart of a child, the rod of discipline will drive it far from him."

Proverbs 29:15 (ESV) — "The rod and reproof give wisdom, but a child left to himself brings shame to his mother."

We couldn't ignore these verses anymore. We had to believe that God knew something we didn't. We had to step out in faith and obedience and start disciplining our child. And by discipline, I mean spanking. We realized that when they were young, the main form of discipline should be spanking, according to the Bible. Proverbs 13:24 (KJ2000) says, "But he who loves him disciplines early." The key word there is *early*. While still young, while there is hope and a lot of time.

"Early obedience has all Scripture on its side." —J. C. RYLE

Obedience can be learned, but it has to be taught. As Christian parents, we are called to show our child the error in their ways and to administer discipline biblically. But how? Where were my husband and I to begin? We felt like we were being asked by the Lord to begin disciplining our son how He intended, despite our feelings and fears.

"My duty is never measured by what I feel is within my power to do but by what God's grace makes possible for me. And I never can know fully how much grace will enable me to do until I begin." —ANDREW MURRAY

We just had to begin. By faith. Praying and asking that the Lord would lead us. Believing His grace was in ample supply and ready to be given out freely to us. We were constantly watching and talking to other families who were also trying to obey Scripture in this area. If the Lord has asked us to do something, surely He will grant the ability to carry it out. Surely He'll grant wisdom and discernment to the parent who is crying out for it. Certainly the Lord wouldn't ask us to do something that would harm our children.

It takes faith to believe these things, though. It takes a first, single step of obedience. So, we began. And so began the doubts and fears that come right alongside obedience. Isn't that so frustrating, how the evil one knows how to discourage obedience by tempting you with fears? When we listen to what Satan says, we say things like:

- "This doesn't seem to be working."
- "Maybe we are doing this wrong."
- "Spanking doesn't work on my child."

It's not that spanking doesn't work on my child. It's that I, as the parent, am not spanking the right way or that I have given up too soon. As strong as that may sound, I believe it wholeheartedly. The other option is that God is a liar, and I can't believe that for a second. Deuteronomy 8:6 (NIV) says, "Observe the commands of the Lord your God, walking in obedience to him and revering him." I have to believe that the fault is with me, or that I have to persist and persevere.

PARENTING DIFFERENTLY

A quote from a booklet published back in the sixties titled *Children—Fun or Frenzy?* by Al Fabrizio says, "Nowhere in Scripture does the Lord qualify His command (on discipline) on the basis of personality." He wouldn't give a command on parenting that only applies to a certain percentage of children. His command on discipline is for all of us, and we need to be confident and determined to obey what is being asked of us without making excuses or giving into our fears. We can't be picking and choosing certain verses in the Bible to obey and leaving out the ones that make us uncomfortable. Where's our faith displayed if that's how we live life?

In a day and age where people are so against biblical doctrine and standards, it's up to Christian families like us to live boldly and by faith, knowing that this kind of living will look differently from the rest of the world. The Lord has asked us to parent differently, and He's given us the freedom to say no to Him and His manual. But at what cost? What (or who) will we be forfeiting by doing things our way?

My parents chose to parent differently. They lovingly chose to discipline their seven children. They chose not to leave us to our naturally flawed tendencies but to help correct and direct us down the right path. It didn't ruin us or make us aggressive or even destroy our relationship with our parents. My six siblings and I have an amazing relationship with our parents and adore them, and we believe that their obeying the Word and disciplining us through spanking has helped shape us into the Christian adults we all are today. I'm living proof, and I wasn't the easiest kid to raise.

I knew it then, and I can see it now that I have children of my own.

Sometimes in the heat of the hard season, we can be tempted to think that these biblical methods don't work. At one point, I thought that too. I was pregnant with my fourth son, and my other boys were five, four, and two. I've never experienced such exhaustion as I did that summer. I was feeling very spent mentally, physically, and emotionally.

I always seemed to skip that cute, small pregnant stage. I always went from throwing up and being extremely sick for the first twenty weeks to huge and swollen and growing at an exponential rate. I was tired all the time, and I would wake up from a full night's sleep feeling exhausted. You know, the mind-numbing tired.

At this same time, my two-year-old thought it would be a good idea to start waking up in the morning screaming. I'm talking, the "I'm angry at the world" screaming. There wasn't a reason why, but every morning, this was my reality. Then, to my husband's and my horror, the morning screaming turned into temper tantrums throughout the day. My husband and I knew pretty quickly that we had to address this.

Our kid was getting out of control.

I had to recognize that when he started his early-morning screaming, that was the beginning of my work for the day in disciplining my son's wrong behavior. He'd wake up and begin screaming. I'd waddle into his room and pick him up from his crib as he was still screaming at me. Slowly, I'd lower myself into the rocking chair in his room, carefully lay him across my lap (I didn't have much of a lap anymore at that point because of the size of my pregnant belly), and I'd give him a spanking. I'd then hug him and hush his crying and comfort him.

But sometimes he didn't want to stop screaming, and I hadn't been consistent enough yet to show him that when "Mama says no screaming," she's going to follow through with discipline if he didn't obey. I had to continue being consistent every single morning.

I had to show my little man that Mama meant what she said. I had to be more determined, more stubborn than him.

Do you know how many mornings I had to remind myself of the truth regarding discipline?

"Discipline your children, and they will give you peace; they will bring you the delights you desire" (Proverbs 29:17, NIV).

Daily and hourly!

Because it didn't seem or look or feel like my spanking him was accomplishing anything. I was constantly praying for evidence of the fruit of my labor in my son, that he would obey and learn. I could've probably ignored the fact that he screamed every morning, his temper tantrum flaring. I could've probably distracted him with a Pop-Tart and cartoons in the morning to get him to stop, but I couldn't quiet down the Holy Spirit urging me to address my son's sin.

"Beware of letting small faults pass unnoticed under the idea if 'it is a little one.' There are no little things in training children; all are important. Little weeds need plucking up as much as any. Leave them alone, and they will soon be great." —J. C. Ryle

I believed this then, and I still do now. By faith, if we are putting forth the effort to raise our children how the Bible instructs and commands us to, I have to believe there will be fruit. I've experienced it with my two-year-old mentioned above.

His dad and I won that very long battle. We kept with it even though it took a long time; it took countless mornings obeying our Heavenly Father.

My son Mack no longer throws temper tantrums or screams in the morning. He is such a joy to us. If you're lucky enough, maybe you could experience a "Macky hug," the best kind of hug. It's earth-shattering and neck-breaking. Even though we had a really rough, long season with this kid, he loves us more than ever. He knows that Mom and Dad are in charge, and when he doesn't obey, he gets spanked. It's not a big deal because that's what he knows to be true. He doesn't doubt our love for him, and he's slowly learning that God is in charge of everyone and everything. He's learning that because we're showing him.

"Reader, if there be any point which deserves your attention, believe me, it is this one. It is one that will give you trouble, I know. But if you do not take trouble with your children when they are young, they will give you trouble when they are old. Choose which you prefer." —J. C. Ryle

Now that we have had kids for eight years, we know discipline doesn't automatically mean a spanking every time for disobedience. Our hope is that we put in the work and effort when they were young so that as they grow up, the spankings lessen. We now have more conversations with them and different forms of discipline. We are just broadening this different season of parenting. But the work begins when they are young and needing you constantly. It also makes sense that we need our Lord constantly to show us how He intended us to bring up our children—His way, not ours.

ACTION TIPS:

- Read the book of Proverbs and then read it again.
- Make a choice to either obey your Heavenly Father and to administer discipline His way or to do it your way. Through faith we obey what He tells us to do. Do you need to start obeying your Heavenly Father in this area?

4

HIS DAY VERSUS MY DAY

"Take my love, my Lord, I pour, at Thy feet its treasure-store. Take myself and I will be, ever, only, all for Thee."

—Frances Ridley Havergal

Every pregnancy, as soon as week four, nausea would set in and so would begin my mothering from the couch or my bed or not at all. Whenever my husband could get off early from work, he'd come home and I'd go to bed until the next morning just to start all over again. Sometimes, my sisters or mom would be able to come and help for the day. They'd cook, do laundry, clean out my fridge, and raise my boys while I was just trying to survive the day. (I never told them this, but whenever they would drive away at the end of the day to go back to their lives, to their own homes, to their own cities, I'd cry. They brought a certain comfort to my heart and home that is indescribable.)

Just survive the day. That would be my motto for the first seventeen weeks of each pregnancy. *Just make it through this day.*

Now that I have my four sons, it seems my responsibilities

outside of "just pure survival" have grown. It's taking care of four high-energy boys (who are constantly running and eating), being a pastor's wife (who is responsible for helping run different areas of ministry), and choosing to homeschool these boys (whose great idea was that?). And also, running a home and all that entails. Now, I find my motto is "just survive this *hour*."

I can feel completely depleted of mental capacity by the time it's 9:30 a.m. That's probably because I have early risers as kids (they get it from their dad, and I blame him entirely for this) or a toddler who likes to wake up screaming and raging at the world and ready to battle at the awful hour of 6:00 a.m. Breakfast hasn't even been started, and you still need to get a full day of school in. Rinse, repeat.

Let me say this on those "just trying to survive" days: we need to just stop. Just stop the train. Let the older kids go play for a bit, pick up the screaming toddler, and talk to your Heavenly Father—really talk to Him. Cry if you need to. But talk to Him. Invite Him into your morning and allow God to take over. Audibly give Him the remaining twelve hours in your day. Plead with Him to redeem this day and to direct your thoughts and actions.

"The King's heart is a stream of water in the hand of the Lord, He turns it wherever He will." —Proverbs 21:1 (ESV)

Do I give God the freedom to handle my day? If we aren't constantly pleading with the Lord to intercede on our behalf, asking Him what He would have us do next, if we aren't asking Him to open our eyes to the conversations He wants us to have with our children, don't we run the risk of missing Him and missing "it?" "It" being His design for my day. His day as opposed to my day. His words He wanted me to communicate with my children as opposed to my words.

Most days, I do the exact same things, whether I'm in line with His will or not. Some days, I sort laundry, cook (even if on those days, it's frozen pizza, which is still considered cooking, right?), homeschool, and referee my children's lives. But when it's a day ordained by my Heavenly Father, and I'm constantly asking Him if this is where He wants me today, the difference is that *His* day bears fruit. His day is full of peace. Mine isn't. His day is full of the same struggles as my day holds, but I rest assured in His will and sovereignty.

When I'm faced with a six-year-old and his sour attitude, I can believe God led me there to help my son learn how to say no to his poor attitude. When I hear, for the hundredth time, my two-year-old screaming and throwing a temper tantrum, I know God brought me there to repeatedly, lovingly correct that outburst. When I see tears of confusion from my four-year-old because he can't articulate what he's feeling and what's going on in that amazing brain of his, I know God is there with me. He led me to be there *for* my son and *with* my son, helping him, teaching him, and guiding him.

There's purpose behind God's leading. Whether or not I give Him permission to take over my day is completely up to me. When the only sounds in your home lately are screaming or crying, and it's not just the kids, make sure your screaming and crying are toward your Heavenly Father for His strength. If you look anywhere else, you're going to be discouraged. If you look to anyone else, you're going to be disappointed. We need to be crying out to the One who put us here, the One who has appointed us our work.

WHAT'S NEXT, LORD?

A common phrase in our home is, "What's next, Mom?" My boys have learned that when it's chore time, or when I tell them we have work to do, they have to go do the chore I've given them. When it's done, they come find me and ask, "What's next, Mom?" Is this how I am with the Designer of my day? Am I continually asking Him, "What's next, Lord?"

I love the verses Psalm 123:1–2 (ESV): "To you I lift up my eyes, O you who are enthroned in the heavens! Behold, as the eyes of servants look to the hand of their master, as the eyes of a maidservant to the hand of her mistress, so our eyes look to the LORD our God." I love the picture of the maid looking to her mistress as if asking, "What's next?" I love picturing myself as that maid looking to God throughout my day, asking Him, "What's next, Father?" It becomes His day as opposed to my day.

I remember there was one Sunday in particular *when everyone (myself included) just seemed so off. We had arrived home from church, which then usually begins our favorite time of the week: Sunday football! But on this day, everyone was arguing. Fighting and selfishness were rampant. There was whining, no matter the age. I was losing patience and raised my voice many times. I was actually yelling. There seemed to be a tension between my husband and me even though we were both supposed to be on the same team.*

These days aren't meant to happen on a Sunday; these days are reserved for a Monday or any other day that's not on the weekend. I was crawling into bed that night upset, not super pleased with how I handled all the poor attitudes. I know I missed out on some good teaching opportunities with my sons. But I had to go to sleep and rest on the assurance that the grace and forgiveness I was craving was readily available to me. I had to grab hold of it and plead that tomorrow, when all this sin tries to rear its ugly head again, I'd be ready.

Sometimes, I think you need to have the lame Sundays filled with grace and forgiveness to appreciate the brand-new Monday that's coming with no mistakes in it yet. The Monday that can still be given over to the Lord to run it. Certain nights I'm lying in bed so grateful for His mercies (sometimes, those mercies are that the day ended), and that He has tomorrow set up for me to try again. So, I'm clinging to that hope that lies in tomorrow, and I'm clinging to the One who set it there.

Champion

5

IT IS ALL ABOUT ME!

"If the God of nature has created her for a calling, and the God of grace has redeemed her to fulfill that calling in the interests of His kingdom, she assuredly may trust His power and love not to forsake her in her hour of need."

—Andrew Murray

Being a mother, I can be so focused on what changes need to be made in my children, what areas my kids need to grow in. I can be so focused on their weaknesses and sins that I forget that God wants to use those weak areas in my children's lives to grow and stretch me. God wants to be refining me, growing me first—or at least laterally—with my kids. More than a handful of times, I've been going through a difficult season with a child, and I get discouraged and beat down because of their behavior and sin.

Because of the character struggle raging in my child's life, it can so often bring to the surface an area in my character the Lord wants to address. It's like I have a "lightbulb moment" in the midst of the struggle with my child, and suddenly, I see what the Lord has been trying to communicate with me. God is constantly using my child's sin to bring to the surface the areas in my own life that need to change. Yes, He wants me to address sin in my child's life, but He also has His eye on my growth as I lead my child in the growth of their character.

Do I really believe that battling my fifteen-month-old to stay in bed at night for up to three hours a night for over a year was meant for my growth as much as my child's?

I would do myself a great service to believe it and realize it while I'm going through this turbulent season with my child. "What are you wanting me to learn here, Lord?" I could ask. "What would you have me grow in, Father?"

One thing I seem to learn over and over again is that the Lord wants me to get it first. He wants to teach me something through every struggle and trial. He has something specific He wants me to learn. Maybe He's just waiting for me to submit to His refinement. His refinement is my growth, and it's how I'll change.

THIS SEASON'S HARVEST

You may be tired and discouraged with the behavior of your child. I understand that. It's easy to see the behavior and sin and forget to hope that there's growth happening even when it isn't visible at the moment. Galatians 6:9 (NLT) says, "So let's not get tired of doing what is good. At just the right time we will reap a harvest of blessing if we don't give up." In due season. We don't determine the length of the trying season with a child. We can't force them to get it or speed up their obedience. We have to trust the One who is in charge of the seasons we are in. Not every season is harvest season. There has to be a lot of work and preparation before we can harvest, or even see the evidence of a harvest to come. There's a season of sowing seeds in our children accompanied by prayer. There's a season of maintaining those planted seeds, reinforcing them, watering them—again, always accompanied by prayer.

Lately, when I've been going through a tough season with a child or even dealing with areas in my life that I know I need to change in, I've been asking the Lord for evidence of growth. Just a glimpse of the fruit that is to come. Sometimes, the Lord says yes, and I see evidence of my hard work, which spurs me on. Other times, He says, "Daughter, continue by faith. Even when you can't see anything happening." And then we can have hope that in God's timing and sovereignty, we will see a great harvest in our lives and the lives of our children. But the harvest date is not set by us, and we can't grow weary while working for a harvest. *Don't give up! Friend, meet Him there in your child's struggle. Chances are He's got His eye on you, and He's asking you to grow as well.*

When we believe that the Lord wants to grow us, and believe that our children can often be the curriculum used to teach us exactly what the Lord would teach us, our day can be covered in peace. Does that mean your kids' deliberate sins won't wear on you anymore? No, not necessarily. Growth in your kids can be just as painful and uncomfortable as your own. It also means that it can give the Lord incredible freedom to make known to you exactly the area He has for your refinement—your refinement and your child's. Rarely have I seen my children make huge steps in character growth without learning something myself. I grow and change alongside them.

I remember thinking often when I had a couple toddlers underfoot that I was never an angry person until I had children. I was never a yeller until kids came along. I was a pretty patient person who rarely got frustrated until I had children. I would also think, *As soon as they are old enough to do some things by themselves, I know I won't be so short and harsh with my words.* I'd even think, *As soon as the baby is sleeping through the night or when I'm done being pregnant and not so exhausted, then this sin of mine is going to magically disappear.* Well, sadly, it didn't. How I wish that were the case.

Our children are just bringing out which sin is lurking in our hearts. Can children magnify and intensify our weaknesses? Absolutely. But don't be making excuses for your sin and thinking that all you need is time and more comfortable circumstances, and then your sin will be gone. This is why I believe God is asking you to grow and change just as much as your children.

If only we wouldn't hide or shy away from the heat of the fire that's meant to bring us out refined and have the course grittiness burned away. Like Proverbs 25:4 (NLT) says, "Remove the impurities from silver, and the sterling will be ready for the silversmith." Don't flee the fire of refinement. It's meant to burn away the impurities that the Lord wishes to remove from us! If only we would embrace His refining. Even though His refinement can be uncomfortable, we keep believing it's for our good. He wishes to use us even more. The more we become like His Son, the more we can have a greater impact.

You may want a break from life, like being able to go to the grocery store without someone throwing a temper tantrum. You may want to go right to bed at night and not have to discipline your toddler for hours, teaching them to stay in bed. Maybe you're wishing and hoping for the day when mealtime isn't like World War III, and everyone peacefully eats what you just spent an hour making. I feel you all. Just don't give up. Don't disengage and raise the white flag of surrender. Our children need moms who are more stubborn than they are. Moms who are more determined to train godliness rather than leaving their children to themselves.

God sees the struggle, and He is orchestrating everything you and your child need to grow. Don't fight His design. Settle into the struggle, gripping desperately, white-knuckled onto the peace that God offers. Right in the eye of the storm, you can find your Father offering His hand, ready to help you through the tilling seasons if you allow Him to.

"Beware of the thing of which you say—'Oh, that does not matter much.' The fact that it does not matter much to you may mean that it matters a very great deal to God. Nothing is a light matter with a child of God."
—Oswald Chambers, *My Utmost for His Highest*

ACTION TIPS:

- Recognize the areas of sin in your own life that are brought to the surface when your child is sinning. Does your child's sinful behavior bring out fits of anger and rage and harsh words? Or does it bring out fears and anxieties? Identify it, call it what it is, and, with the Lord's help, be growing right alongside your child.
- Don't grow discouraged by all of the loud sin that's in your child and you. Remember there are seasons in life and every season has its purpose. Don't try to skip the growing seasons. Rely on your Lord's strength and allow Him to be growing and changing you and your children.

6

NOT A MORNING PERSON

"Strength of my heart, I need not fail, not mine to fear but to obey. With such a Leader, who could quail? Thou art as Thou wert yesterday. Strength of my heart, I rest in Thee, fulfill Thy purposes through me."

—Amy Carmichael

Imagine this. You wake one morning feeling rested from your uninterrupted night's sleep. Your coffee is strong and hot and waiting for you. You get to have a great quiet time before any of the kids wake up. Plus, the sun is shining! Wow! This is shaping up to be a good day. You're feeling encouraged with life and with your role as a mom and feeling pretty darn good at the moment.

But then, the baby wakes up screaming.

Which wakes up the toddler, who then has a grumpy attitude, and the other kids can see how the morning is going, so they follow suit and have grumpy attitudes as well.

That hot cup of coffee you were just sipping on goes cold and tastes bitter, and suddenly, the sun is gone and here come the rainclouds.

What happened to your wonderful morning you were just having? Suddenly, you don't feel so encouraged with life. Maybe you're not doing so great at this mothering thing, either, so it's probably best if you just have a bad attitude as well.

So quickly our circumstances can change, which can then affect our feelings about ourselves or our kids or our role as a mother. But the truth is, we can't be mothers by our feelings, especially on those days when the coffee tastes bitter instead of delicious. We can't parent by our feelings because they can be so easily swayed and can switch on a dime.

I'm not who you would consider a morning person. Never have been, never will be. But my kids don't know that. They need a mom who's ready to receive them whenever the day begins. No matter the hour. No matter how I feel about mornings. I can let my feelings immediately be thrown off course because of my situation, or I can take hold of my feelings and put them to death right there at the coffee pot. I can reroute my heart and my feelings instead of letting them continue down the path they've begun on.

Why should I battle my feelings? Often, my feelings like to focus on myself. And being focused on yourself while trying to mother well isn't going to produce lasting fruit in your life or your children's lives. Let's first talk about how we battle against ourselves. Sometimes that battle rages all day long. And sometimes you never really feel like you've won because you're struggling all gloomy day long to enjoy your little people or be content with this calling of motherhood. The point, though, is that we choose to engage in the battle against our feelings and stay engaged as long as necessary.

But how? How do we put these feelings to death? These feelings of discontentment, anger, discouragement, grumpiness, or my ever-present struggle against a bad attitude, topped off with a mighty dose of irritation. All these feelings don't help us mother better.

Most of the feelings I struggle with on a daily basis are focused on me. To myself, I am very evidently a selfish person. You may be able to relate to me in this area or maybe not. But what are we doing to fight against these unwanted feelings?

WINNING THE BATTLE

The battle is won through prayer. I've had days that started with an amazing quiet time in the morning with my Savior. But then, I remained in the battle against myself through prayer, constantly crying out to the Lord, asking for His encouragement, truth, and strength, asking for Him to change the feelings I was battling against, persevering with my requests through the rain and gloom. Sometimes, I need to blast some worship music to help minister to my feelings, to help put them in their place. Is that corny or cliché? Maybe. But I've found it helps me. Sometimes, I will gather up the kids, and we'll sit down together and talk about what we have all been struggling with that morning. Then, we pray for each other. Together, we pray against the feelings of selfishness, meanness, or laziness. Whatever we've been struggling with, I try to help them recognize it and then pray against it. As moms, we can recognize quickly how our day is going, and we have the ability to stop it in its track and ask the Lord to reroute our day.

> *"The highest condition of the human will is when, not seeing God, not seeming to grasp Him at all, we yet hold Him fast."*
> —George MacDonald

We may not feel God in our day or feel like He's answering our prayers, but hold on to truth. The truth being, He sees you. He hears you. Trust Him when your feelings breathe lies. Even though I've experienced all-day struggles, sometimes with the Lord's divine intervention (I don't use that term lightly, either), my attitude, my feelings, and my heart follow my fervent prayers. But if I'm not focusing my mind and heart on something other than myself and my feelings, then chances are I'm going to stay right where I'm at in my gloomy, rainy state.

Let's not allow our circumstances to rule our outlook on the day. "This is the day the Lord has made I will rejoice and be glad in it" (Psalm 118:24, NKJV). Do we believe that? Do we believe every aspect of our day is allowed or ordained by our Heavenly Father? Do I believe that maybe there's a bigger reason behind my seven-year-old's grumpy attitude? Maybe God wants to address something in my heart in the morning, and He knows *exactly* what to use in my life to bring it to the surface: my children.

FEELINGS, BEWARE!

Just like how we need to be speaking truth into our kids' lives, we need to do the speaking of truth into our own lives and not allow our feelings to be the driver of our days. "The heart is deceitful above all things" (Jeremiah 17:9, NIV). If you believe that, as a Christian, you never need to instruct your heart and reboot the way it's feeling, or that your feelings can't be used against you as much as they can be used for good, then I would say your heart is being deceived.

How do you feel about your calling as a mom? Have these things ever crossed your mind?

- I feel discontent, like I'm missing out on my purpose in life.
- I'm on the brink of being resentful because I don't feel

fulfilled or even feel like I'm losing who I really am, who I was before I had kids.
- I'm looking for things or people or business opportunities outside of my home to help me feel better about myself.

If you can say yes to one of these things, you should feel good about yourself, because I've said yes to all of them. I've been there. I've sumo wrestled God with His calling for me to be a full-time mom at home. Why? Because being home caused all these feelings and lies to prickle up in the back of my head—feelings I didn't like and lies I didn't want to believe.

SUPER MOM

Back in the first years of motherhood, I was pretty proud of the fact that I was juggling so many irons in the fire. I had a small hair-styling business that I was running out of my home, and I was meeting up with women daily. We had a steady flow of roommates living with us, so my home was always full of people. I was having playdates with other moms and adventures with my two little boys, because at the end of the day, I felt productive. I couldn't just be a stay-at-home mom, could I? How old-fashioned! What was I contributing to our life? What would everyone think I did all day? And what about my personality? I like to be busy, always running around, living by no schedule but the one I chose for that day. Does this mean any of those busy things are bad? Absolutely not.

I'd hear about moms who had been in the mom game longer than I, and how they couldn't do much in the afternoons because their youngest kids napped. They always tried to be home so they could have their naps, and I would smile sympathetically while thinking, *Oh, that poor woman. She should be a little more flexible. I'm not going to let my kids dictate my schedule. My kids will learn to be flexible.* Never mind the fact that my two children were borderline terroristic.

In my humble opinion, the heart behind that busyness is what turns it into discontentment. If I'm feeling bored or stir-crazy, not wanting to let go of my other dreams, and if my toddler is out of control and my baby is following closely, then maybe I need to reshift my priorities to focus on the feelings behind my busyness and character training. Maybe your feelings are leading you in the wrong direction. Again, these busy things aren't bad, but maybe you should take an honest evaluation of the state of your home and children, the condition of your marriage, and, most importantly, your walk with the Lord. Ask yourself these questions:

- How involved am I in my local church?
- Am I giving my home priority?
- How is my marriage?
- How is my children's behavior? Do they obey me? Do they seem peaceful?
- Do any of these areas need work?
- What can I, as the main runner of the home, cut out?
- What are my feelings behind all these "things" that I'm doing?

Proverbs 31:27 (NIV) says, "She watches over the affairs of her household and does not eat the bread of idleness." I remember reading this verse during this period of my life with a bunch of young children gathered around my legs and being convicted that this Proverbs 31 woman probably had to be home to watch over her household. She had her eye on her household, and she wasn't idle while at home. If I had a day at home with no real plans, oh man, I was lucky if I even got out of my pajamas that day. And the kids? The only changing of clothes for them would be into fresh pajamas right before their dad got home in the evening.

Why such the struggle to be busy while at home? Being home and idle, which is just a nice word for lazy, is obviously mentioned in Proverbs 31, so it's a real thing. For me, it was pretty simple because there was no one watching me at home except for my kids. Somewhere along the way, we believed the lie and the feeling that our work at home is less fulfilling than a career. Why is that? Because it doesn't invigorate me or excite me? Wiping bums and putting Band-Aids on scrapes doesn't feel as important as a career? I feel you. Staying at home can feel like the very opposite of important. It can be lonely and discouraging, mind-numbingly tiring, thankless, and unnoticed. Why would I put myself in this situation if I can escape it?

So here I was feeling convicted about being home more, feeling content with mothering in my home, living by a schedule for the sake of my kids' peace of mind and my sanity. I was also conflicted with the seventeen verses before verse 27 in Proverbs 31, which talk about everything that the mother and wife did, all the work she did for her family, and all of the different hats she wore. She helped provide for her family, after all.

Quietly, the Lord suggested to me, "Why don't you let me show you what you should be doing?" Now there was a thought. I heard it. I had to try it. So I started slashing things out of my schedule left and right. I couldn't maintain this level of busyness. My children were suffering because of it. I was neglecting the most important work assigned to me: their character. I knew what Titus 2 said to young women about loving their husbands and children, to be self-controlled and pure, to be busy at home. Oh, I knew this, but did I believe this was actually for the best? Did I believe that verse was for me?

Titus is telling older women to teach and show younger women to be busy at home, so it's not always a natural, pre-programmed instinct the moment we bring that first baby home. Eventually, I took a brutally honest evaluation of my walk with the Lord and the behavior and condition of my two little children and admitted, "I need to try something different because what I'm doing isn't producing the results I desire in myself and my little tribe." So what did I do? I stopped running my hair-styling business in my home, even if it meant losing the extra cash I was earning. I stopped meeting with girls regularly, giving priority to my toddlers.

"Lord, you have assigned me my portion and my cup, you have made my lot secure. The boundary lines have fallen for me in pleasant places, surely I have a delightful inheritance."
—Psalm 16:5–6 (NIV)

This verse above has been such an amazing soundboard for me with mothering. Am I putting my energy and efforts toward His assignment for me, or am I pouring myself out on what I feel like I want to be doing? He has an assignment for us. In the few years we have our kids in our home, God has His assignment papers already written for us! Are you willing to ask for them, or are you content with your own agenda?

"Don't bother giving God instructions; just report for duty."
—Corrie ten Boom

Also, realize that different stages of mom life require different degrees of intense work. Granted, I've only reached to age eight with my oldest, but where I'm at now is very different from where I was four years ago. I'm sleeping through the nights, mostly uninterrupted. I'm not pregnant or nursing anyone. No one is in diapers, and everyone can feed themselves. My daily life changed quickly over the last four long years of pregnancies, infants, and toddlers, and now the Lord is again quietly suggesting to me, "What if I showed you what I want you to do?"

It's a completely different assignment but with the same theme:

your character and your children's character. Learning to be content at home. Working hard and faithfully at my home address. It's the same theme and the same juggling act—just a different season of life.

There's no way I could've been working on writing four years ago while also mothering well. I'm thankful I gave the Lord permission to "set my task before me." I'm glad I finally took my assignment papers from Him, and that He spared me from myself and what I may have felt I should be doing. I know fully well that sometimes what He asks me to do doesn't always feel like what I want to be doing in the beginning. But somewhere along the way, He is so faithful to grant a glimpse of affirmation that when we follow His plan for our lives, it's worth it.

ACTION TIPS:

- Your feelings in the midst of drudgery and monotony or conflict and correction—are they bringing you into closer communion with your Savior and your children? Or are they distancing you from them? If they're distancing you from them, with the Lord's help, harness them, wrangle them, and redirect them.
- Look at your weekly schedule. What is it filled with? Take a look at your heart behind your schedule. Evaluate if you're running your home and children from a place of peace and contentment, or if you're doing things stemmed from something the Lord wants to address.

7

OUR GREENHOUSES

"Quality time can never substitute for ordinary days spent, doing ordinary things, together."

—Elisabeth Elliot

It's 5:45 a.m. Another brand-new day lies before me. I can almost tell you exactly what every hour of my day is going to look like, because every day before this one has looked the same as the one before. Life is pretty simple around these parts. It's the same routine day in and day out. Every night, before Shane and I fall asleep, I ask him what he has going on the next day. After he tells me, he jokingly asks me what I have going on. I say "jokingly" because we both know that Monday through Thursday, my days will look the same.

I rarely leave the house unless it's in the evening for a church meeting or wrestling practice, and in that case, it's a family affair. But during the week, I'm home. We have our routine, our schedule, and my weekly things to get done. My boys have their list of the same chores to do every day of every week. Going into my week with the mentality of "I'm going to be home and work hard" helps wire my heart to be content with what the Lord has asked me to do.

I'm to be home and be attentive to the mundane tasks of mothering, being the main caretaker, the captain of the mother ship, and the leader of my troops.

It wasn't always this way, though. I was messaging one of my older sisters the other day, and we were talking and laughing about how this is our reality. Our days and weeks look the same, rooted at home, teaching (a lot of teaching), with the same daily routine. But not that long ago, I wasn't laughing about this. No, I was kicking and screaming and fighting this reality with all my might. I saw and felt my world starting to shrink smaller and smaller with the more babies I had. I felt like I was also shrinking from the world's notice. I was losing my freedoms, and I was neglecting friendships. I missed the days of being carefree, setting my own schedule on my own terms, and not having stretch marks or torn abs from carrying Hulk-size babies.

Fast-forward a few more years, and my world is even tinier and wrapped up in my pint-size humans. So how did I fight this unwanted disappearing act from the world's eyes? I scheduled things. Playdates, mom groups, zoo trips, children's museum outings. I met moms at the mall play area, the library, and the park. Anything to get me out of the house! Anything to keep these feelings of insignificance at bay. Anything to fight this boredom I would feel with my role as a mom.

You may be thinking, *Yeah? So what? Is that a bad thing to be doing and scheduling all those things?* Good Lord, no! It most definitely is not wrong. But I was challenged with this thought from the Lord, addressing what was going on in my own heart. *What if the Lord wants my world to shrink? What if the shrinking is His doing? What if a teeny tiny world with a kid wrapped around each leg is His plan?*

The Lord started shifting my thinking when my babies miraculously turned into toddlers who liked to get their own way. They also liked to display their very loud, selfish tendencies. Oh, and they were highly opinionated. They couldn't communicate super well yet, mind you, but they didn't need words to share their opinions. They seemed to notice that when we left the house, Mom wasn't going to discipline them for wrong behavior. She brought loads of snacks that she readily offered whenever the smallest fussing or whining occurred. They noticed I'd give them anything they wanted so they wouldn't throw a temper tantrum or interrupt my conversation with the other lady who was doing the same thing with her kid.

Could we possibly, sometimes, have a skewed view on the familiarity of our homes and the slow, not-so-exciting pace that we usually find there? What if we viewed our homes as a greenhouse? A greenhouse for our little seedlings as opposed to a place of only mundane tasks and boredom. This greenhouse was specifically designed for you and given to you so you could reap the highest harvest possible. This is where we focus on our seedlings, including their character and natural tendencies. Here, we can assess what each seedling needs or is lacking. In this safe place, we can give discipline when discipline is needed. Those outbursts that happen in the grocery store line also happen at home, don't they? Those blatant sins that our amazing children like to show off while out in public are most likely occurring in our homes as well.

In my experience with my kids, their public behavior is often an overflow of what I'm either doing or not doing at home.

"Children watch for the weak spots on the battle lines. If they find they can get away with things in the grocery store, in the car, or at Granny's house, they will certainly avail themselves of the opportunities."

—Elisabeth Elliot

You've experienced this, right? Oh man, I have. These kids are smart. They can smell fear a mile away, and they smell it on you when they begin screaming in the grocery aisle. They know that panicky look we get when they begin fussing in the play area. Be encouraged! The Lord has given us the time, the tools, and the place to address these things.

But are we too busy? Always gone from our homes? Too distracted? Our homes are the best battleground—I mean, training ground—for our seedlings. If we are constantly removing our little seedlings from their greenhouses, aren't we doing everyone a disservice? Why are we constantly packing our schedules to the gills? For a change of scenery? For adult conversations? For distracting our kids? I realized there's always evidence of something going on in myself and my children. It's usually right beneath the surface, or it broke the surface and is very apparent.

There is evidence of what I'm giving priority to and it's either producing good fruit or there's evidence of little seedlings that need pruning, work, and attention. Very rarely have I ever experienced a time in my life that the Lord wasn't pruning me in some way. He always has His eye on my growth.

"The Lord is more concerned about your character than your comfort."
—Rick Warren

This applies to our children too. He's constantly asking us to grow and mature in some area in our lives. How I love to be able to reflect on what the Lord has taught me in my life, to reflect on how He has pruned it for growth. How encouraging it is to see my life change!

But is that how we view our children? Are we more concerned about their character than their comfort? Are we more concerned about their character than *our* comfort? Do we believe that they need a mom focused on their character and the temperature of their hearts? We need to have a clear vision on the areas in their lives that need pruning, areas that the Lord has made clear to us that He wants us to address with our kids, areas that need our attention. Or maybe the Lord doesn't have to show you anything, because your child's sin is nice and loud.

A clear place to start is to simplify your life, clearing your schedule and focusing in-house. When I actively started to *learn* how to be busy at home and focus on my children's character and my own, I started to see growth in myself, which seemed to trickle its way into my children. Kids aren't going to grow godly character unless you teach them. I started experiencing growth that could only come from a teeny tiny world with God and me as I clung to Him. Yes, I have my days when I don't welcome the familiar simplicity that has become my life; but when those days come, I'm gently reminded of my purpose. I'm their mom, and I'm responsible for training their character. And then I'm nudged to keep at it because it's worth it.

I'm still learning to lean into the struggle and not run from it kicking and screaming. I'm still learning not to escape the work that comes with having a greenhouse. Just because we have a greenhouse doesn't mean we will automatically reap the harvest we want. We have to be willing to put in the work the way the Lord has designed the work to be done. Welcome the shrinking world because God is there and He sees us.

That being said, does this mean we never leave the house during the week? Am I encouraging you to live the life of a hermit, completely antisocial and focused 100 percent of the time on your children at home? Heavens, no! The Lord wants us to be focused on people, loving those in our neighborhoods, churches, and community. The Lord wants fellowship for us moms. He knows how it can encourage us. My favorite kind of encouragement comes from one mom to another as we sit down on the carpet of a living room, with babies lying between us and toddlers running around. It's the sweetest fellowship I've known in this season of my life. I've learned to be very intentional with those scheduled times, because as sweet as they are, they don't happen very often. The Lord has asked me to win with my little people. They can lose ground so quickly if I'm not engaged with them at home first.

FINDING THE BALANCE

Before I was homeschooling my sons and only had toddlers and babies, I limited myself to one fun outing a week with a mom friend. That was it, and that turned out to be enough. Being involved with my local church also gave me ample opportunities to get out of the house and experience fellowship. If I was also going to small group or house church or a prayer meeting or service project, I was seeing people throughout the entire week while also showing my sons the priorities in their parents' lives.

Is Mom so tired from all of the activities this week that she isn't able to go with Dad to small group? Or to the monthly women's meeting at church? It's almost like God was asking me, "How many times have you been to the park or zoo this month? And how many times have you been to small group this month?" I didn't like my answer. I was so busy with good and fun things that I was too exhausted to make it to the most important things, the ones that help shape our family. Our kids aren't dumb. They see what we make as our priority. So far in my experience, the Lord has yet to ask me to give more of my time to others outside of walls of my home than to those who call me Mom.

Being a pastor's wife for the last couple of years, the pull that comes from others, ministries, and activities is stronger than ever. They're all good things, of course, but do I believe that better things need my attention at home? Think about the job you had before you were a mom or maybe your current job. Think about when you quit or if you were to quit. You were probably replaced in a week or maybe two. That company was still able to run without you. Why? Because you were replaceable there. Now think about your role as a mom. To your kids, you are not so easily replaceable, are you?

Now let me be so bold to say this "everything" that you give your time and mental energy to (that isn't your husband, your children, and your home) has some degree of effect. Some things have small effects; some have big effects. Think about the mental effort that weekly meal planning takes. Or the concentration that's required for making a grocery list.

Yes, these are small tasks that have a small effect on our lives and our children's lives. But you need at least a couple uninterrupted minutes to do that. So you have all these small in-house tasks that need your daily attention, physically and mentally. Then you have the needs of your husband and your relationship with him. More things to mentally and physically account for. Then comes each child and all of their struggles and needs. That can take up a lot of mental concentration and being led by the Spirit.

These kids of ours need our undivided attention. In a perfect world, we could give them that. But even if we're doing the bare minimum in life, we still need to give our attention elsewhere at certain points. I haven't even begun talking about if you're going to homeschool your kids.

That enters you into this whole new realm of mental exertion. But now moms also want to be doing all of these things outside the home. Physically and mentally, we can't do it all. We weren't meant to. God didn't call us to. Someone or something is going to get the short end of the stick from us. Someone or something is going to get our leftovers.

Today, it's like women are truly starting to believe they should be able to do it all. Their own agenda and God's agenda. We are meant to do the work the Lord has for us today as a wife and a mom. This is His curriculum to refine your character and to make Himself known to your children.

"The homemaker has the ultimate career. All other careers exist for one purpose only—and that is to support the ultimate career."
—C. S. Lewis

I remember when I was trying to live my life being a mom but also living out my own agenda. And very quickly it was evident that who suffered the most was my kids. I wasn't able to devote most of my time and energy into the molding of their character; in fact, I wasn't really even thinking about their character. I was too busy trying to be "time efficient" and getting everything done and checked off my to-do list to even think and meditate on what the Lord would have me do with my kids. I was surviving. I was willfully allowing myself to be pulled in a hundred directions physically and mentally. I realized this pretty quickly and saw clearly that my home wasn't peaceful. One of the big contributing factors to that was my fighting against God's design and calling in my life.

What did I do? I had to submit and simplify my life. I had to submit to God's calling for me and His agenda. I accepted that friendships couldn't be a priority—even ministry had to be less on my list. Playdates, workout regimen, hobbies, and business adventures had to take their rightful place: beneath my calling at home. The peace that came with that realization was incredible.

This can be highly controversial, I know. I think it's because for some of us, we think that staying home doesn't fit our personality. You think you would go crazy at home all day. Well, it's not about you. The minute that first baby exited your body and you became a mom, life ceased to be about you and your preferences. Actually, life should never be about you and your preferences. The minute you chose to bring a child into the world, God assigned you His calling.

Motherhood. And if you are His daughter, then that calling is extended to you.

This shouldn't feel unfair or feel like a trap. This should be so peaceful knowing that God has given this same calling to thousands of your Christian sisters. We don't have to figure out the other callings and purposes in life in addition to motherhood. We can peacefully rest in the assurance that God doesn't ask you to focus very far beyond your front doorstep. He's given us a mighty task, an honorable commission in our homes. It's our own agenda that looks beyond that for more. Focusing on your home and your kids and what the Lord may have for you right there at your home address is fulfilling despite what the world tells us.

"Children are not a distraction from more important work. They are the most important work."
—C. S. Lewis

I'm not saying we can't do anything beyond being a wife and a mom. (Even though that is completely and absolutely fulfilling). Writing this book took over a year—and it also took a lot of work and mental concentration. It took juggling schedules with my husband and me that I could get alone and write; but the difference I'm talking about is if the Lord is leading you into work outside of your home, you can be assured that His blessing will follow. It's because we're living out His agenda and not our own. If we are faithful with the many little things we have to do at home, God adds to our plate by His design. And it's covered in peace. I'm determined to *learn* how to be content and *learn* how to do my work of mothering well at home, not in a mall play area. I thought only a certain personality of a mom could be content and joyful staying at home. But then I realized the things that reflect my Heavenly Father don't come naturally to me, either. I'm not supposed to make exceptions, though. I'm supposed to work at it and learn how to be content and joyful at home.

Once I realized what the Lord was asking of me, and I made a change of removing those distractions that took me outside my home, I was instantly filled with peace. Instantly! The battle between the two wills was finally over: my will for my own way and my Heavenly Father's will for His way for me. Even now, years later with older kids, I have to be aware of how busy I can be outside my greenhouse, and I'm extremely protective of it. I believe those early years of your child's life are so important for this greenhouse mentality to teach the right behavior.

Thankfully, my eight-year-old doesn't throw temper tantrums as he did at fifteen months, but I didn't teach him that at the park. It took months of staying consistent at home disciplining that wrong behavior. So now that my little spirited toddlers have been trained not to scream, cry, and fall to the ground when they want something, we have more peace to leave our house on a whim. It's still a rarity, honestly, but I do believe it's because the work has been done in their early years. I'm trusting it's going to follow them even into their teen years and adult years.

Annoyingly, distractions still try to sneak their way into my home, but if I'm resounded in my conviction that the Lord wants me staked out in my greenhouse, I can resist the outside pulls. Nehemiah 6:3 (ESV) says, "So I sent messengers to them, saying 'I am doing a great work and cannot come down. Why should my work stop while I leave it and come down to you?'" Nehemiah wasn't willing to be distracted from his work, assigned to him by the Lord. And what was he doing? He was building a wall. What's so great about that? If the Lord has assigned work to you, it's urgent work and it's vital that you do it. Nehemiah clearly caught that. But is that how we feel about the work happening in our homes or not happening in our homes? Could we, maybe, be escaping the very place God was hoping He'd find us so He could meet us there? I'm learning when I finally submit my desires, ideals, and expectations to the Creator, I land smack-dab in the middle of His design, and there happens to be enough peace for every mom who, by faith, chooses to be there.

> *"Home is the place where habits are formed, home is the place where the foundations of character are laid, home gives the bias to our tastes and likings and opinions. See then, I pray you, that there be careful training at home."*
>
> —J. C. RYLE

ABORT! EVERYONE BACK INSIDE!

There was one day I remember well. From the moment everyone woke up, there was fussing. There were bad attitudes all around. Everyone was just about the most annoying person to everyone else. I remember thinking multiple times, *We just need to get out of this house*. Now don't get me wrong, because there have been plenty of times we've escaped our four walls for an impromptu donut run or a quick trip down to the gas station for a giant slushy. But on this day, I ordered everyone outside for a walk through our neighborhood. *We just need some fresh air and sunshine,* I wistfully thought.

After everyone's shoes were found (miraculously), sweatshirts were dug up, and the baby was put in the stroller, I triumphantly exited our house. We didn't get past our driveway before the first meltdown occurred. *Really? Couldn't we at least get past the neighbor's house?* But I was determined. *We just need this fresh air!* I thought.

The walk didn't have the effect I was hoping for—at all. By the time we went around the block and came back up our driveway, the baby was screaming and struggling to escape his stroller restraints. I was dragging one son, who was sure he dropped his treasured rock three-fourths of the way back. One kid was bleeding, and I wasn't entirely sure when or how that happened. And the other one was walking beside me, grumbling about how horrible this walk was. We all returned to our home with the same horrible attitudes. I just happened to put them all on public display for the whole neighbored to see, and I put too much expectation on that fresh air to make a difference.

A change of scenery isn't going to change the issues of the heart. It may distract, and it may prolong the inevitable, but the behavior of our kids and ourselves are going to change when we allow it to be brought up and clearly shown and addressed. As the moms, we get a clear, front-row view of these little people and the sin deeply rooted in them. I have yet to experience any sort of character growth in my little people outside the four walls of my home. God has given us all our own little greenhouses with our own little plants. What a blessing! Maybe you need to stop viewing your home as a place to escape and believe that in the home is where the real work is done.

"In this little time does it matter, as we work, and we watch and we wait. If we're filling the place He assigns us, be it labor small or great."
—Author Unknown

ACTION TIPS:

- Assess your weekly schedule. How full is it with things outside of your home? Could the Lord want to change that so you would give more priority to character growth in your kids at home? Fewer distractions for you and your kids is the goal. And more clarity for areas in your lives that need to be addressed.

- Evaluate the temperature of your heart toward the area of being content and fulfilled with being "just a mom." Does the idea make your blood boil? Does it make the hair on your arms stand up? I challenge you to search the Word and prayerfully ask the Lord to show you if He has an opinion on this topic for your life. He won't be silent! No matter His answer to you.

8

PRAYERS AT MY KITCHEN SINK

"JESUS, SAVIOR, DOST THOU SEE?

When I'm doing work for Thee?
Common things, not great and grand
Carrying stones and earth and sand?
I did common work, you know,
Many, many years ago,
And I don't forget. I see.
Everything you do for Me."

—Amy Carmichael

I've probably clocked in hours upon hours that have added up to days standing at my sink washing dishes. I was thinking the other day about how the space between my sink and kitchen counter has felt thousands of my footsteps, preparing three meals a day at least five to six days a week for the last eight years. That's a lot of standing and walking in one place. About a year ago, I started to be mindful about the time I spent in my kitchen and how I could be intentional with my time there. My time cooking for my family and washing dishes could also be a time when I'm communicating with the Manager of my day.

While I'm standing at the sink, I try to pray and talk to my Lord. I pray through my prayer list for my burdens, my worries, my kids, my husband, my attitude at the moment, and my regrets about my behavior. If you're like me, you have a couple of kids with constant questions and needs interrupting your prayers, but our Lord doesn't mind. He is patient and waits for us to get back to our conversation. My prayers at the sink are usually accompanied by a toddler sitting on the counter next to me, chattering away. But we're moms, and multitasking is our jam. I can do it well.

As moms, I don't think we can fall into the trap that our times spent in the Word or in prayer have to look like it did before we had kids. I have little humans that require my attention all the time, and I can't just decide, "This morning, I'm going to have an extended time with the Lord!" Being a mom of babies and toddlers, we don't have that freedom in this season of life. For the last eight years, I've had more fast and furious times in the Word than long, deep, extended ones. That's just my reality, and that's probably your reality as a mom. Let's not limit the Lord speaking to us in only ideal circumstances (like an absolutely quiet house) and moments. We need to be desperate and creative with our times with the Lord but also show priority. A quick ten minutes in the Word is better than nothing at all. Interrupted prayers at the sink are better than no prayers at all.

"Is prayer your steering wheel or your spare tire?"
—Corrie ten Boom

Corrie reminds me to ensure I'm making prayer a priority in my life. Do I find myself only praying when I'm desperate? I was convicted to take my thoughts captive and be more intentional with the times I let my mind run wild. Why don't I pray instead?

Back when I had nursing babies, and I was up multiple times

during the night, waking up early to have quiet time was out of the question. I would have to find time during my day to meet with the Lord. Before I knew it, my day was over and I hadn't been in the Word at all. How did that happen? Well, I was keeping multiple humans alive. When would I find the time to read His Word? It would seem I didn't have any left. That, of course, wasn't true. If I had time to check Instagram multiple times a day, then I had time to be with God. I was simply using it elsewhere.

Then one day, I had a thought. *I have to feed this baby multiple times a day. I'm required to be in somewhat of a sitting position for that. Why don't I read while feeding my child? Instead of scrolling through social media, why not read?* Was it interrupted by my non-nursing children? Absolutely. But isn't interrupted reading better than none at all? I found even through those interrupted times of reading that the Lord still wanted to meet me there on the couch. He gave me just what I needed in the limited time I had. I was showing the Lord my relationship with Him was a priority. I was still trying to be in the Word, hearing from Him. I was praying to Him while at my sink, serving my family.

For you moms who are in the throes of babies and toddlers and up multiple times a night with a newborn, that season changes. Before you know it, that newborn is sleeping longer stretches at night. You're feeling a little bit more human in the mornings, and that's when maybe it's time to start setting your alarm twenty minutes before the baby usually wakes up. You turn the coffee maker to auto brew the night before so your coffee is hot and waiting for you (if you don't have an auto brew, they're very affordable). You dive into the Word desperately and expectantly to hear from your Lord this morning, eager for Him to give you some truth to carry you through your long day. And then you fervently pray for ten minutes, knowing this is the most important communication you will have all day long.

At some point in our day, we need to be intentionally positioning ourselves in front of our Father's heavenly throne to hear from Him. We can't use the excuse that we don't have time. We have time, but maybe we're not using it wisely. You can be creative in this stage of life. Where in your house are you spending the most time? In front of your kitchen sink? On your couch nursing for the hundredth time that day? At your kitchen table teaching your children to read? How can you bring the Lord into those days when you feel aimless, unmotivated, and disengaged with a to-do list a mile long? You've started some things on your list half-heartedly, but you finished nothing. You feel like you're limping along in your mothering, not really doing the quality job you know you should be, and your relationship with your Savior is less than ideal.

It's almost like you're just waiting for something to spark some life into your home and some motivation in your parenting. Perhaps you need a spark in your spiritual life. You're waiting. Not sure for what, but maybe it's more like hoping that your feelings will align with your calling in life. Mothering. Not just mothering, but godly mothering. For this, always run to the Word. It speaks truth when your feelings try to breathe lies.

Recently, I was reminded of the importance of always going to the Word for truth as opposed to accepting my thoughts and feelings as truth. I was helping my eight-year-old son learn something new in his math lesson that day. Here I was pretty confident I knew what I was doing while explaining to him how to divide and what to do if you have a remainder. I was certain I remembered how to do this. I was feeling confident and good about myself! But even though I was fairly sure what I was saying was right, wouldn't it be wise of me to check the answer key just to make sure? This is the same with us and how we can feel confident in what we think we know, but unless we're checking the answer key (aka the Bible), our thinking could be wrong. I would never intentionally teach my son the wrong way to do division. But I don't know what I don't know until I know it. And we learn the truth from our answer keys, the Bible. We should be checking our thoughts and what we believe according to Scripture.

Spend intentional time in prayer. Prioritize your relationship with the Lord and see what He does.

"The unfolding of Your Words give light:
it gives understanding to the simple."
—Psalm 119:130 (NIV)

There are so many times I feel simple or in over my head with all I've been asked to do by my Heavenly Father, but He says, "My words give understanding." We need to be in the Word daily, knowing that the only wisdom we truly need is found between those pages. We can't rely on those "verse a day" apps or even a two-minute devotional. That won't cut it. We need to remember that in our prayers is where battles are fought, strength is granted, and guidance is given. In God's Word, wisdom is delivered and endurance is handed out. But why do we think we're going to be given any of those things without asking for them? My mom used to say to me when I had a baby on my hip, a toddler around my legs, and a new one growing in my belly that "short, desperate prayers are as effective as long prayers." I've clung to that these last eight years of mothering. And I've uttered short, quick, desperate, and heartfelt prayers.

"Prayer is one great secret of spiritual prosperity. When there is much private communion with God, your soul will grow like the grass after rain; when there is little, all will be at a stand-still; you will barely keep your soul alive. Show me a growing Christian, a going-forward Christian, a strong Christian, a flourishing Christian, and sure am I, he is one that speaks often with his Lord. He asks much, and he has much. He tells Jesus everything, and so he always knows how to act." —J. C. Ryle

"I take refuge in the fact that while I don't know everything, I do know Someone who does."

—A. W. Tozer

ACTION TIPS:

- You have twenty to thirty minutes a day to be in the Word and pray. I promise you do. Find it. Protect it. Intentionally meet your Lord there. He's always waiting.
- Have someone keep you accountable with being in the Word daily. Even if it's your husband asking you when he gets home from work at night. Maybe if you haven't found those twenty minutes during the day, you could sneak away for a quick twenty-minute feast on the Word before you feed supper to your family. Make it happen. Be desperate to hear from your Lord; He doesn't care what time of day you meet with Him.

9

SIMPLE PLAY

"Some ol-fashioned things like fresh air and sunshine are hard to beat."

—Laura Ingalls Wilder

My sons were born with two speeds. Slow, which only happens when they are sleeping or sick. And fast. Most of the day, they are stuck in the fast gear. The energy levels in my home can be exhausting, and the noise level is deafening. The amount of testosterone flowing between my four walls in my home is, as you can imagine, always at an all-time high.

Our dinner table is one of my favorite places. We all sit-ish (I say "sit-ish" because we tell them about a hundred times a meal to sit on their bum) together around our table, and we eat, talk, and laugh. It never lasts as long I want.

"The sun looks down on nothing half so good as a household laughing together over a meal." —C. S. Lewis

But someday, our dinnertime will be longer than fifteen to twenty minutes because no one will be in a race to scarf down their food and get back to their playtime. We'll linger at the table and enjoy each other's presence even more, and we'll replay our days, bringing everyone up to speed on life. My second born will undoubtedly say something funny and make everyone laugh, as he does so well. My oldest will share a fond, not-so-long-ago memory that will involve people we love, and he'll bring us all into that memory with him because he remembers little details. My third born will share something that he picked up on by just observing those around him, and we'll all listen in amazement at how his mind works. My youngest will say something as well. Actually, he'll shout it because he's the youngest, and he'll need to use a louder voice to be heard over the noise; but we'll all catch a glimpse of his curly hair and stop talking immediately. Once again, he'll have all our attention for a brief moment. My husband and I will sit there and listen to our sons talking and laughing, and our hearts will be filled to the point of bursting. We won't have to tell anyone to "eat the food on your plate" or to "sit down."

Someday, I believe this will happen, but today is not that day. Our days are filled with noise and constant movement. They're filled with nonstop coaching, correcting, and comforting. They're filled with putting out fires, metaphorically and literally. Each day is a balancing act between drawing them outside of their heads and getting a glimpse of what's going on in their hearts. I spend much of my time answering requests with a "yes" or a "no" or shouting out a warning with a "stop that" or a "just be careful" while choosing to look away. My parenting can be so influenced by my preferences, biased opinions, and fears.

Is that all a bad thing? No, not necessarily, but I would offer a word of caution with parenting only by our preferences. For example, I prefer the noise level in my home to be somewhat quiet, or at least at a respectable decibel level. But my Lord gave me four boys who are loud and very full of life! Their loudness isn't foolishness or fighting or disobedience. It's just how God has deemed fit to wire them.

They are just playing together and doing it loudly. Do I tell them to be quiet because I'm annoyed with the noise level and that goes against my preference? To be fair, we do teach our boys that there is a time and a place to be quiet and still. We teach them that there is a time and a place for wrestling and being rough with each other, and that it isn't in the aisles of Walmart or church or church meetings. (You may be shocked how many times I've said "no wrestling" while at Walmart.) Isn't the time and place for them to do these things in our home—despite what our own personal preferences or biases are? And you may answer that question with a resounding "No! Not in our homes, either!" I understand the struggle. But if your children are anything like mine, they were born with a God-given amount of energy, and if they aren't able to have a release of that energy, for my boys at least, the result is foolishness. God has wired our children in very specific ways, unique ways, and if we say no to those wirings in our kids because it's outside of what we're comfortable with, then I think we are in real danger of our kids not growing into the men and women God has in mind for them.

I don't ever want them to resort to foolishness if I can help it, so we've made our home a safe environment for wrestling and rolling on the ground and for tickle fests. I've put my preferences aside for the sake of my children. My preference would be that my kids don't make such a mess with scissors and cutting up paper, so do I ban scissors from our home? Of course not. I don't ever want them to break a bone or get hurt, so do I tell them to stop the wrestling, play-fighting, fence-walking, and tree-climbing? Do I forbid them from the puddle of water they found in the backyard? Do I say no to anything that is going to cause them to get dirty, or that I have to clean up?

I know all you moms out there have something or someplace or activity that is strictly on your blacklist. But why? Let's explore this further.

I've had people in my home I don't know very well, and they see how my boys live life and how we run our home. Some have said, "Hannah, you are the perfect boy mom; you are so laid-back!" Little do they know I wasn't always this kind of mom. I liked making sure my day was *not* filled with any unnecessary work, messes, or extra stress. The more children I had, the more I realized I could either fill my days with entertaining them on my terms and level of messiness that I was comfortable with, or I could let them use their imaginations and play the way God had wired them. Does this mean I give them free rein, and they get to do anything they want? Do I allow them to jump on couches, run through the house yelling and screaming, and act wild and disrespectful? No, definitely not. But we do let them climb, balance, fall, dig, get muddy, and play freely. For kids to play this way, they need freedom from their parents. They make messes, but then they help me clean up. I teach them how to clean up; it's not just Mom following behind them cleaning up after them.

I've seen an adventurous spirit grow in my sons with the more freedom I gave them in their play. The more I stopped fearing a mess or a broken bone, the more they tried new things and came up with new ideas. They truly take ownership of their play. These are the kind of men I hope to raise: godly, adventurous, and spirited men!

Maybe your kids have figured out how to laugh quietly and yell softly during their play, but mine haven't. As soon as I want to yell downstairs, I'm constantly asking myself, "Are they being foolish, or are they just loud because they are kids having fun?" I need to listen for foolishness or disobedience before I stop them. Sometimes, I'll yell down a reminder not to get foolish, but other times, I'm pleasantly surprised and let them continue. Other times, I look outside and see them doing things that immediately spike my blood pressure, like boosting each other up to a higher branch in their favorite climbing tree. I have to stop and ask myself, "Is what they are doing dangerous or adventurous?" And really, what kind of adventure doesn't come with some sort of risk? Other times, I've looked outside and seen one son chasing another with a sledgehammer slung over his shoulder. Dangerous? Unwise? Yes! I'd say that falls into those categories. So, naturally, I stop it and tell that son of mine it's not wise and to put the sledgehammer away.

Today, I know some children are growing up without that sense of adventure or drive to experience new things. Our culture is raising our children in front of screens all day, labeling it "screen time." How many times do we parents see our child bored, and instead of encouraging them to go play, we give them a handheld device or the remote to turn on Netflix or their favorite YouTube channels? All this time spent with screens leaves children abandoning their imaginations, seldom finding themselves bored or in need of using their little brains to keep themselves busy. We are robbing our kids of the opportunity to get lost in a game they came up with all on their own. We are keeping them from the scars acquired from a fully active childhood. In a culture of overprotective parents, we need to be different because the ones who are going to be hurt in the end are our kids themselves.

THE LOST ART OF PLAYING OUTSIDE

Thinking back on my childhood, we always lived on an acreage with land all around us. Some of my favorite memories are playing outside with my siblings, making forts in the woods behind our home, or exploring the junk pile for treasure (along with carcasses of small animals. Bones were always the prized treasure). We climbed trees as high as we dared, raced on our bikes to see who could make the longest skid marks on our gravel road, collected walnuts from our walnut tree, and battled each other. In the winter, we made hay bale forts in our barn loft (our dad was never pleased, but I don't recall him ever stopping us). In the dead of summer when the corn in the fields was far above our heads, we'd play hide-and-go-seek among the stalks or a game of Marco Polo where the only way we could find each other was throwing ears of corn into the air as a signal of our location. Oh, the fun we had on that acreage!

I also don't ever recall my mom or dad telling us we *had* to go play outside—that's where we *wanted* to play. If we were bored with our toys inside, the only other option was to go outside. We weren't allowed to watch TV during the day except for an hour in the afternoon when the house was supposed to be quiet for our younger siblings who were napping. We had a computer and a Sega Genesis saved for Saturday and Sunday afternoons after church and work.

Is it safe to say we are losing this kind of play as a culture? We are losing the ability to use our imaginations or the fine art of simple play. I know not all of us live on an acreage with barns, woods, and cornfields around us to encourage our children to play outside. We are surrounded by neighbors on a cul-de-sac with busy streets. I get it. That is currently our situation. In our case, it does take more effort because we need to be creative and take the initiative.

My husband and I have been amazed at the ideas our boys come up with when we give them the freedom to use our backyard for play. It means saying yes to climbing a tree, digging a hole, walking on the top of a fence, and getting outside with them and teaching them how to ride a bike or throw a ball. It takes work. It takes us, as the parents, to initiate and encourage them. I'm convinced that when God had the idea of trees and envisioned their purposes, He intended that they would function as His very own, custom-designed playgrounds for children. It's in our kids' DNA to climb a tree, so let them!

WHAT ARE YOU GROWING IN YOUR YARD?

My husband loves to have a good-looking lawn. He loves how a well-kept, maintained lawn looks and feels under bare feet. During the early spring months, he will over-seed and fertilize the lawn, aerate our yard, and put down grub killer and insect killer. He waters it religiously and weeds it tirelessly. When he mows, it's in perfectly straight lines. Understandably, the pull of keeping a beautiful lawn with the wear and tear that four boys can do always competes against each other. To remind each other when we're conflicted with saying yes or no to our boys playing in the backyard, we remember a quote: "We are raising kids, not grass." It's a reminder to hold loosely to our material things and preferences and remember our priorities. My husband and my preference would be a beautifully manicured lawn that has landscaping that would get hundreds of saves if it were on Pinterest. But we also want our boys to be active outside so we have had to put those preferences aside and fill our backyard with things that encourage kids to play. We've had to save our pennies to buy playsets. We've watched Craigslist like hawks for things we can get for our boys to play with outside. We are not going to have an empty, beautiful square yard and expect them to enjoy it. It takes initiation, time, and sometimes money to get your kids to love something. And encouragement. A lot of that.

> *"Happy hearts and happy faces. Happy plays in grassy spaces. That is how in ancient ages children grew to kings and sages."*
> —Robert Louis Stevenson

My children are not perfect. They are so far from perfect, but they also aren't out of control. They are busy and full of life. We correct and discipline foolishness always. And rowdiness when it's in the wrong setting. My husband and I are trying to teach them what is wise play and what isn't. There have been times they bring tools and scrap wood out of the garage, and they have an idea to build something amazing. I can either let them try or tell them to put it away because this could end badly, knowing they could smash a finger with a hammer. Yes, all of that is true, but I'm certainly glad this isn't how God treats me in my daily life. I'm so thankful He gives me the freedom to try new things and sometimes fail or make a mess.

You may be a fear-prone mama, and the sight or even thought of your child doing anything that could result in an injury prompts you to say, "Stop!" Maybe, instead, hold your hand over your mouth, say a quick prayer, and let your child try it. And when they fall and scrape their knees, you can teach them that they are going to be okay. In a culture that's enabling fears and overprotectiveness, that waves the red flag at every worst-case scenario, let's be different and trust our sovereign Lord, who is in control of all things—our children included—and let our children be children.

"Trust Him when dark doubts assail thee,
Trust Him when thy faith is small,
Trust Him when to simply trust Him,
Seems the hardest thing of all."
—Keswick Hymn Book

ACTION TIPS:

- Assess honestly what is on your blacklist with things your children can and can't do. Are you saying no to things based on preference or fears?
- Turn off all screens and get your kids outside! (Try going a week with no screen time.) Encourage them to enjoy the outside. Help them come up with ideas of what to play. Think about the games you loved to play as a kid and show your kids how to play them. It will be hard for them to learn to love being outside if you're inside sitting on the couch.

10

SLOW SOWING YEARS

"I have rightfully no other business each day but to do God's work as a servant, constantly regarding His pleasure. May I have grace to live above every human motive, simply with God and to God."

—Henry Martyn

It seemed like just yesterday everyone was still in diapers and unable to make coherent sentences. My days were mainly just survival mode, trying to keep everyone alive and fed. Trying to keep them on something that resembled somewhat of a schedule. My goal was to teach them how to take naps when I told them it was naptime and how to sleep through the night and mostly on their own (did you know you can actually teach them to do that?). Or how *not* to throw temper tantrums at the sound of the word *no*. How to obey my simple commands. You know, important survival stuff. Things they should be taught when transitioning from baby to toddler.

Then one day, you realize you're also in charge of teaching this little human how to use the toilet and you start researching how to skip the toddler stage altogether. But I swear one day they all wake up in the morning and walk out of their bedrooms half dressed with their adorable bedhead hair that should've been washed two days ago, and you realize everyone is older. Like a lot older. Everyone can somewhat dress themselves, everyone can feed themselves, everyone is talking and has opinions. They usually always use the toilet now, much to everyone's pleasure! (And there was much rejoicing!) My panicky "I'm going down and taking the ship with me" feeling is not so constant anymore. I promise it's like it happens over the weekend.

But now that my kids aren't all just babies and toddlers anymore, the Lord brought to mind that just like I've had to lead and show my children the necessities of a good and healthy lifestyle, I also had to begin showing them the necessary habits of a Christian. A Christian living a life yielded to God. The practicals. The habits. Am I showing them *how* to have a relationship with the Lord? Am I giving them all the tools they need to hear from the Lord? Am I helping them form good habits before they even realize or acknowledge the value in them?

The Lord has reminded me I have a choice every hour of every day to either do this or not. This being, do I bring these children of mine into my day or keep them out of my way? Instead of keeping them out of my hair or keeping them distracted, am I bringing them alongside me and seeking out their heart? I've been realizing the difference in the caliber of my days when I'm being intentional with my sons. But why? Why is this important?

LEADING BY EXAMPLE

Imagine with me your favorite celebrity pop singer is preparing for her multimillion, worldwide tour. She's hired her backup dancers and her backup singers, and now rehearsals have begun. She's hoping and counting on these individuals to fulfill their role as her dancers and singers. Now imagine she and her coordinators give no direction at all to these individuals. They don't set up rehearsal times or encourage them to be practicing. Nope. They just hope they learn how to do the dances and how to sing the songs just by being in the vicinity. In fact, they can be as distracted as they want to be because it keeps the noise level down so at least the pop singer can get her work in. They'll figure out how to do all the dance moves for all the songs even though they aren't being shown how, right? They should turn out to be great dancers and backup singers, right? They should get it, right?!

Do you see the absurdity here?

I know this is a silly metaphor, but I think it's seriously sobering if we as Christian moms hope that even if we don't show our children how to live the life of a Christian, somehow they are going to just pick up on it. Just because they live in a Christian home does not mean they are going to know and learn how to live the way God wants them to—unless we are intentionally showing them.

Whenever I read Deuteronomy 6 (NIV), I'm equally convicted and spurred on by the charge to us parents.

> “Love the Lord your God with all your heart and with all your soul and with all your strength. These Commandments that I give you today are to be upon your hearts. Impress them on your children. Talk about them when you sit at home and when you walk along the road, when you lie down and when you get up. Tie them as symbol on your hands and bind them on your foreheads. Write them on the doorframes of your houses and on your gates.

Is that how I view my time with my children throughout my day? Am I looking for opportunities to talk to my kids about the love that

God has for them? Am I taking the time to impress on my kids the importance of obeying God?

Are we teaching our children the whys and hows to live this Christian life, or are we just hoping for the best? Are we practicing with our kids daily how to have a relationship with our Savior? Pleading with the Lord that someday our Savior will be their Savior, or are we just hoping that through our distracted lives they'll see what we're doing and just pick up on it and hopefully want it? Is that the risk we're willing to take with our children?

Are we leading them in prayer? Teaching them how to pray and why we pray? Are we leading them through the Word and instilling truth? How about memorizing Scripture? Are we being disciplined enough to take the time to lead them in memorizing Scripture? I've had to pray and pray and ask and ask the Lord to show me when I can lead in these areas with my kids, because it takes time to stop your day and sit and lead.

SPIRITUAL PRACTICALS

Not long ago when my boys weren't reading well enough on their own, I found that having this time of reading the Word and memorizing and praying worked well before we started school every morning. So (mostly) every morning, I would have my four sons sitting at the dining room table with the youngest usually in my lap and I'd read a chapter from the Bible from whatever book we were reading through. Afterward, we'd talk about what we just read. Sometimes, there was a lot of discussion that came up; other times, there wasn't much chatter and we would move on to whatever verses we were memorizing.

After our memorizing, all of us would then pray for our day and pray for people we wanted to see get saved and pray for the things in our life we knew the Lord wanted us to change in.

It didn't always go perfectly and it wasn't always super smooth, but I believed there would be fruit from it eventually. The hour before we started school undoubtedly was the most important hour in my day.

This is urgent business, after all. Billy Graham said,

> "Only God Himself fully appreciates the influence of a Christian mother in the molding of character in her children."

I believe this with my whole heart, but if I'm not doing practical things preceded by fervent prayer, aren't I just rolling the dice and taking my chances? This is one of the main reasons we have cut out all TV/tablets/Netflix from our daily lives. We only allow these things on Saturdays and Sundays during the school year. (Don't get me wrong. I can binge on Netflix like the best of them.)

My husband and I realized a while ago how quickly and how often we would willingly choose to allow our kids to be distracted as opposed to dealing with behavior and character issues. Turn on Netflix, and everyone is quiet and calm! It seemed peaceful, but for us, all we were doing was ignoring whatever issue or disobedience had surfaced.

Now, instead of watching a show before bed, I read a book to them and then my husband will work on memory verses and pray with them and put them to bed. That has been a true picture of peace for us. Conversations being had, hearts being heard, fears being calmed, dreams being shared.

Don't opt for distractions if the Lord has put an issue on the front burner for you to deal with. Don't forfeit opportunities to lead your children into communication with the Lord or forfeit positioning them before the throne.

In her book, *The Shaping of a Christian Family,* Elisabeth Elliot talks about the daily practices her parents put in place her whole life and the importance of them. Here's what she says:

> No one can make a child love anything, from spinach to sparrows to Scripture, but the parent's love for things exerta powerful thrust in that direction. We learned, finally, to love the Bible, in spite of all the years when we shrugged and sighed and rolled our eyes and poked each other under the table during devotions and generally appeared to ignore what was supposed to be going on. Much more than we or our parents knew sank in by a sort of providential osmosis.[1]

Does that give you hope like it does me? Even when it doesn't seem like anything is sinking in. If we are faithfully taking the time to lead our children to the cross, if we are constantly directing their eyes up by pointing to the One who was hanging on that cross, it's going to be worth it in the end.

WORK/CHORES PRACTICALS

We want hardworking, disciplined children, right? But what are we doing on a daily basis to train them to turn out that way? Let's talk about the importance of teaching our children to not only work, but also to work hard. I know the struggle of just wanting them busy and peacefully playing together so I can plow through my to-do list instead of showing them how to work alongside me. We can lack in teaching. We can lack in bringing them along.

One thing I've learned is when my kids are with me in a project, there's so much talking going on. We're working together. Raking a yard. Stacking firewood. Unloading a dishwasher. Folding laundry. Scrubbing floors. We're together working because I intentionally brought them there by my side. I'm hopefully doing two things: 1) showing them how to work and 2) showing that I'm also being intentional with my conversations. While we are working together, I can bring up what we read in the Bible that morning, or using that togetherness to fill up their love tanks by being affirming with my words toward them. I might bring up something I know they thought was funny from the other day purely for the fact of laughing and working together. But my favorite thing to do while working together is blast our favorite worship music (or sometimes our favorite pop song) and together sing at the top of our lungs. Letting the Spirit lead me as I lead them in work. Knowing that there are two kinds of work being done at that moment, and one is exceptionally more important than the other.

Have you ever tried to show a two-year-old how to start doing chorus? Or even remind your eight-year-old the standard of work you have in your home? This can take a lot of time, physically and mentally. It requires plenty of patience and showing them again and again how hard work looks. Especially if it's a chore they don't like doing. But isn't it a lot of little by little sowing every day that we hope adds up to a great harvest by the time they reach age eighteen and leave us? I'm constantly amazed at the amount of work a six- and eight-year-old can do. It's a very rare occasion that I vacuum in my house or sweep a floor or unload my dishwasher anymore. Making beds and picking up bedrooms isn't my job anymore; it's their job now. But that's only because I slowly had to intentionally put responsibilities on their plates.

My three-year-old isn't exempt from work, either. He's become a pro at gathering trash cans on trash day, or lining up shoes in our entryway and picking up toys right alongside his big brothers. But in order for this work to happen, I need to be intentional and disciplined to show them how to do the work and then *ask* them to do the work. Then I need to make sure they're actually doing the work and doing it well with a good attitude. This can take time. But if I'm consistent with asking and showing them how it's done, in a couple days, they got it!

"Work hard and become a leader; be lazy and become a slave."
—Proverbs 12:24 (NLT)

Sounds like we definitely want to teach our children to work hard. This does not mean every time I ask them to do a job, they do it cheerfully. So then my job is to address that bad attitude toward work. Does this mean they never quickly shove things under the couch and hope I don't see it? Nope. So then my job is to help remind them the importance of not just getting work done but also doing it well as if we are working for the Lord. Sometimes, it takes hours to get a couple things done because I'm addressing work ethic, heart issues, bad attitudes, laziness, and a slew of other issues all toward work. It can get messy. But do I believe that teaching them to work hard can have eternal value?

"Ordinary work, which is what most of us do most of the time, is ordained by God every bit as much as is the extraordinary. All work done for God is spiritual work and therefore not merely a duty but a holy privilege."
—Elisabeth Elliot, *The Shaping of a Christian Family*

Those simple, mundane things I do daily have a lasting effect. God sees it. Showing and teaching my children that God is pleased when we do the work He has for us well. Asking our kids to come alongside us in our work will by faith have a lasting effect in their lives too. And finally, from Elisabeth Elliot:

> “It is, after all, mostly little, common things that make up our lives. This is the raw material for the spiritual

> life. If we despise small things, regard normal household duties as burdens, routines as boring, rules too confining, we will never learn, nor can we teach our children, to live a life of holy harmony. This takes faithfulness in the troublesome details first of all, learning to do them well that we may make of them an offering to the Lord, for it is His work, after all, given to us.[2]

Don't despise the mundane and let's not neglect teaching our children the blessing and benefit from working hard at what the Lord has given us to do!

"If those who have to bring up children fear too much to cross their inclinations, and so seek always the line of least resistance, teaching lessons only in play, and smoothing over every rough place of the road, the result is a weak, slack will, a mind without power of concentration, and in later life very little resourcefulness in emergency or power of bearing up under difficulties or privations."
—JANET ERSKINE STUART

Let's not shield from our children the things (like character growth through hard work) that God wants to use to help them grow into the adults He wants them to be. I'm trusting my children will look back after they are grown and be so thankful I helped teach them to embrace hard work. We need to welcome these slow sowing years, not try to avoid them. We need to remember these beginning years have a purpose; this is when we lay the foundation of what kind of adults we are raising. Sobering work. But I take comfort in remembering that if God has asked me to do this, He certainly isn't going to leave me alone to figure it out by myself. He'll show us as long as we seek Him out in this area. Seek Him and keep sowing. Slowly yes, but intentionally. Always intentionally.

ACTION TIPS:

- What could you and your husband implement to help your children grow spiritually? Bible reading? Praying throughout the day? Memorizing verses? Family devotions?
- What work around the house could you start showing your children how to do? What responsibilities can you put on their plate? Remember age-appropriate responsibilities. Start simple and keep building

11

THAT'S ALL I GOT

"And our wise Father in heaven knows when we're going to need things too. Don't run out ahead of Him."

—Corrie Ten Boom

"We have here only five loaves of bread and two fish" (Matthew 14:17, NIV).

I remember reading this verse a couple years ago and loved how Jesus went ahead and fed thousands of people with those small, insufficient offerings. He wasn't asking for someone to come and offer a five-course meal they had on hand so He could give that to the massive crowd. No, He asked if anyone had anything to offer Him that He could then use.

How often I feel like what I have to give and offer to my Savior or those around me that need me the most isn't sufficient—it isn't enough. How could what I have to bring to the table possibly be used by my Heavenly Father? I can feel like I'm failing Him miserably, that I've already messed up my sons for sure. But He so gently reminds me of the mighty things He can do when I place small loaves and fish in His hands. When I offer up what I have to Him and say, "Could this be used?" He says it's enough to be used and multiplied. More than enough and then some.

God is able to multiply my meager, human-tainted sacrifices and feed the masses.

These feelings of lacking or not being equipped to complete the task at hand especially arise in the area of homeschooling. My husband and I felt like the Lord wanted me to teach our kids at home. Which is just crazy for me because academics have never been a strength of mine. I don't remember a time as a child not struggling in school, so naturally I can lack in my confidence in this area of teaching. If there's one thing I've learned through teaching my boys at home, it's my confidence in the Lord to show up where I lack.

He takes the few loaves and fish I have to give and He uses them. In fact, He multiplies them. He's able to equip us with exactly what we need to do—not only a good job, but also a great job. Whether it's godly mothering or homeschooling or anything else. I've taken comfort in a verse from Exodus where God is asking for a tabernacle to be built. "I have given skill to all the craftsmen, that they may fashion all that I commanded you" (Exodus 31:6, Berean Study Bible). What a promise! He gives the skill along with the command! Who am I to say I don't have the ability to do something God has clearly asked me to do? If He's asked us to do it, He will see us through it. He'll grant the skills we feel we lack. But isn't that when we need to step out in obedience despite our feelings and believe and trust that God is going to show up?

So often if something is uncomfortable or puts me in a position that I could fail in, I automatically discard it. I'm only on my fourth year of homeschooling, but so far God has shown up and equipped me with exactly what my children have needed. That doesn't mean my schooling looks like it's straight out of a Pinterest picture. Nope. But it's enough.

Your mothering may not look like your fellow mom friends' mothering, but if by faith you are offering up what little you have—or even if it's offering up your empty hands pleading with the Lord to fill them with exactly what's needed to mother well—He'll use 'em. Again and again and again. Just keep offering and asking.

> *"If the Lord fails me this time,*
> *it will be the first time."*
> —George Mueller

God isn't going to fail us. We'll give up before He does. Keep asking for Him to show up when you feel so underqualified for whatever it is He's asking of you. Keep doing the work, reminding yourself that a time of refreshment will come, but also realizing the only way to be refreshed is to do the work.

Why? Because it reveals that I can't do it on my own. I'm not enough without the Lord stepping in and intervening on my behalf. That's when the Lord responds with, "Hey! You are not supposed to be enough. That's my job!"

NOT ENOUGH IS ENOUGH

My son and I share the same dislike of needing help from others. We don't particularly like to be in a situation where we don't know what to do. That's highly uncomfortable for us. It's way too vulnerable for my taste. This son of mine and I have recently come to a situation that naturally would send us running for the hills. It's second grade math. We'd rather push it aside and figure out how to conquer life without it. We'd rather remove anything and everything that stretches us in the smallest of ways because those things (like math) really dampen us from our carefree, laid-back attitudes.

But just like I'm showing my boy that he needs to rely on my knowledge of the math lesson, he needs to trust me and trust that I'm going to help him get through that math lesson of the day. And every day that comes after with math in it. I'll be ready to help him, but he must ask for help. Just like my son, I can't pretend like I have all the means to mother well. Because I don't. Neither do you. In fact, we are severely lacking, and unless we come before our Heavenly Father and admit that we don't have it all together and that we need His help, won't we be just like my son if he just kept pretending like he knew how to do every math lesson ahead of him?

We aren't enough. We never have been, never will be. It can be very uncomfortable consciously walking into something that feels out of your realm of abilities. Just remember being in a vulnerable place with God is just about the safest place you can be—because you are putting all the responsibilities on Him. He's not going to fail you. If the Lord has led you there (like motherhood), believe that He wants to help you carry out that commission well. So stiffen your spine, bend your shoulder to the task at hand, offer up what little you have, and be prepared to be wowed by your Heavenly Father and how He meets you right there.

"A little thing is a little thing, but
faithfulness in the little things is a great thing."
—Hudson Taylor

ACTION TIPS:

- If the Lord is leading you into something that makes you feel uncomfortable and inadequate, don't write Him off. Be excited and follow Him there. He wants to reveal something to you that you experience only when your strength ends and His takes over.
- Recognize the areas in your life that you feel inadequate or weak in. Don't hide them; lay them out before the Lord through prayer and plead with Him to intervene in these areas. And when He does, because He will, give Him all the glory and share with others how He came through for you.

12

THE FRAZZLED LOOK

"I don't believe there are devils enough in hell to pull a boy out of the arms of a godly mother."

—Billy Sunday

You've all seen her. The mom at the zoo surrounded by her little people. Usually, all members of her tribe are under the age of four and half of them are in diapers. She's usually pushing a stroller and has a baby strapped to her. In the span of time it takes for you to walk past her, you hear her tell each toddler, "No, don't touch that!" or "Hey, stay by me and grab the stroller!" or "Johnny, I said no!" or "Suzy, stop pinching your sister!" That span of time was about eight seconds. She may have a scowl on her face and she's got that crazy wild look in her eyes and you can just tell she's frazzled to the core. We've all seen that woman, and we've all sympathized with her. We've all *been* her!

For me, it seemed whenever I went into public with my mighty men, this was the exact picture of me. But the venue I always picked for this to play out was the swimming pool. Taking four boys under the age of six is a questionable decision in itself. But every summer, multiple times a week, I'd pump 'em all up for going to the pool. I'd get them so excited, pack fun snacks, get everyone stripped down to their swimming trunks, and lug them all to the pool. Suddenly, the fun, excited mom who brought them to the pool disappeared and the cranky, snappy, frustrated mom showed up. The balking starts, the commands freely flow without restrain, and suddenly no one is having fun and I turned out to be a liar because I told them how much fun we were going to have. But come on! I'm trying to keep everyone from drowning themselves, or wading away from me into the deep end!

UNREALISTIC EXPECTATIONS

What's the cause of this "not so fun and happy mom" showing up? A lot of times (although it's not always the case), the real problem was I had an expectation that wasn't being met. I had a picture in my head of how our time was going to play out, and as soon as things didn't start lining up like how I wanted, my attitude very quickly changed. How often have plans been thwarted or vacations ruined because I wasn't willing to hold loosely to my ideas, my desires, my control on the situation? I know sometimes disobedient children can wreak havoc on attitudes, but isn't that only because we let them? This requires some major reining in on one's emotions and expectations and crying out for the Lord's help right in the smack-dab middle of that moment.

I've learned while I'm headed out with my sons to go have fun that I need to speak truth to my own heart. Reminding myself, "The kids may act up, but they have sin in them, after all, so be patient and gentle with them when they disobey" or "If we only last an hour here at this place, let it be a fun hour!" or "Lord, show me when it's time to leave." You may be thinking, *You really pray this on the way to the children's museum?* You bet I do! I've learned that my heart toward my children can stay soft and gentle this way instead of being angry and bitter when they ruin my plans. This isn't just positive thinking, either—no, because that's exhausting. This is about your heart and attitude toward disappointments or sinful behavior. One of my favorite quotes is, "The difference between an adventure and ordeal is your attitude."

Remember your kids. Do you want them to remember that whenever they went to fun places Mom wasn't happy unless they acted just like she wanted? She turned into a grumpy commander who gave out orders the entire time. Watch your expectations and attitudes, ladies. It can make all the difference.

My husband loves to camp. In the eight years of us being parents together, we've gone on at least one camping trip a year. Camping with babies while nursing or even pregnant isn't for the faint of heart. Whenever we would be packing up the tent and coolers and pack-and-play, I would always think at least a couple times, *Why are we doing this?*

My preferred vacation is on a beach by a beautiful ocean with a refreshing drink in hand and eating out every meal and doing as little work as possible and getting as tan as possible. But my husband is wired differently, and I have been given four high-energy boys who thrive on active vacations. I knew a bunch of years ago that I could either come alongside my husband and learn how to camp well with our brood, or I could cause a fuss and always send him with the boys on camping trips without me. Through gritted teeth at first, I chose the former option and years down the road, I'm so glad I did. We've had some of our favorite vacations when camping.

Well, except for one . . .

CAMPING TRIP GONE WRONG

One particular camping trip didn't exactly turn out how we expected. We packed up and drove a couple hours down the road to a new camping destination. We hadn't been there a couple hours before I felt a twinge of a headache coming on. I didn't think much about it, but as the minutes passed by, it only intensified. By the afternoon, I crawled into the stifling tent and was trying to sleep this headache off. Of course, I had forgotten to bring any sort of pain medicine for adults, but I had the whole pharmacy for kids packed in the tent. Long story short, the whole afternoon I was nauseatingly trying to cope with and enjoy our camping trip with this full-blown migraine.

Finally, nighttime came around and I was hoping beyond all hope that I would be able to sleep off this migraine. I'm not sure if you've ever slept in a tent on a sleeping bag in the middle of the summer in Nebraska, but the humidity doesn't break much—whether it's two in the afternoon or two in the morning. I couldn't fall asleep. I knew I was dehydrated because my head was only getting worse and literally pulsating with every heartbeat. The vomiting started, the blurry vision ensued, and the groans of "take me now, Lord!" unconsciously escaped my mouth.

Eventually, I got up and left the tent. I knew we had some cans of soda in the cooler and thought putting it on my neck would help the pain. It did help! But as I was sitting in one of our camping chairs by the dying fire with a cold soda can on the back of my neck, three wild raccoons burst out from the nearby bushes fighting and wrestling and snarling at each other. I don't think they even saw me because they tumbled maybe two feet away from my chair.

Well, back in the tent I went.

Somehow, I survived the night only to awaken to a downpour. It was a torrential rainstorm and my poor brain was still trying to explode. That was it. My husband packed us all up in record time.

While I was curled up in a fetal position in the front seat of our van, my boys were laughing at how their dad looked packing up everything in the pouring rain! Not exactly our best vacation ever. Not by a long shot.

Why do I share this story? Do I share it to discourage you from going camping with little kids? Nah, you don't need stories like mine for that—just try it. I share it because my boys are still talking about that vacation as being one of their favorite trips. They remember that it got cut short because of my migraine, but the few things we did with them in those few hours were memorable. We didn't do much more than go on a hike, slop through a mud field, and roast hot dogs and marshmallows over a fire. To them, it was perfect. In my eyes, it was a complete failure. What did they love so much about it? They had Mom and Dad all to themselves, out of our normal element, doing things together. It wasn't extravagant. At all. We can think we need to be constantly having these extravagant experiences for our kids when really all they want is us. They want you undistracted by your phone. Undistracted by other people and work. They want their parents.

Some of our favorite trips have been super last-minute (the Groupon deal was going to expire if we didn't use it soon), like overnight stays in a hotel, swimming in the pool, getting McDonald's for dinner, and watching a movie before bedtime. Easy peasy. Instead of a long, busy, stressful day at the zoo, why not walk to the park with a picnic lunch? They'll remember it and they'll learn to enjoy the simple things in life rather than always expecting big and flashy plans. Trust me, I love the big, flashy plans. (Remember my ideal vacation?) But those don't happen often.

Mamas, don't believe the lie that you need to be constantly creating these big, over-the-top fun experiences. Scale back. Teach them to enjoy the simple things. Simplify. Give them you and your full attention. And who knows? Maybe you'll have a vacation riddled with a migraine being scared half to death by what I'm fairly certain were rabid raccoons. But that vacation could be what hits your kids square in the chest as just what they needed and wanted, after all. I've witnessed how these little but intentional things can create avenues directly to their hearts.

That's what we're after, right? Their hearts.

ACTION TIPS:

- Going into any situation and ask God to help you hold loosely your expectations. Just enjoy your kids.
- Less is more. Keep it simple. They don't care. They just want you. Keep this in mind each day.
- What's something simple you can plan with your kids in the next week? Bonus points if it's free!

13

VOICES

"HE WHO HATH LED WILL LEAD,

All through the wilderness,
He who hath fed will surely feed,
He who hath heard thy cry,
Will never close His ear,
He who hath marked thy faintest sigh
Will not forget thy tear,
He loveth always, faileth never,
So rest on Him today—forever."

—Amy Carmichael

When I was pregnant with my first son, I remember having an almost panicky realization that this baby was coming and I had no idea how to be a mom. I also had this same panicky moment after he was born and we were home from the hospital. My baby didn't know how to nurse and I didn't know how to show him. My dear and wonderful husband didn't know what to do either, so we just kept looking at each other with clueless stares. We didn't want to say out loud that we hadn't the foggiest idea what we were doing. The sleep deprivation was strong, and my emotions and hormones were even stronger. My mom had come over to my house for that first week to help with the baby, and she cooked and cleaned and had me take naps and baths. Amazing, she was truly amazing. But of course, Nana can't stay with us forever. She had to go home, and my husband and I had to figure this out on our own. My mom was driving away from my house, and I was outside on my front porch steps, crying and thinking, *When is this baby's mom gonna show up and take him home? Oh, wait. This baby is never leaving. He's gonna be with me . . . forever.*

And I started crying again.

Those first babies can bring up and out all the emotions and fears. I know. I experienced them head-on. What could I do, though? I had to get up and walk back inside, pick up that baby, and figure it out.

One thing I did purely out of desperation during that time was trying to mimic women around me who were a couple steps ahead of me in life with mothering. Those moms who had three or four kids who clearly had survived the newborn phase three or four times over and who lived to talk about it. I clung to them, honestly. I watched them like hawks. I called them weekly and I sought them out at church. I dropped strong hints about playdates with my newborn purely for the chance to sit at their feet and glean wisdom from them.

But having children wasn't the only requirement they had to meet for me to want to learn from them. These women I was seeking out were all living godly lives. They very clearly had personal relationships with the Lord and they were growing spiritually. They were just a couple skips and jumps ahead of me. Who better to learn from than those who are ahead of you and have figured out something you've yet to learn! I took Psalm 101:6 (NIV) very seriously then, and I try to now still: "My eyes will be on the faithful in the land, that they may dwell with me; the one whose walk is blameless will minister to me."

I was actively seeking out the "faithful and blameless" in my land because I knew I had no clue how to raise babies and I saw these families around me that seemed to have figured out a thing or two. Not just raising babies, but doing it in a godly manner.

Today, we live in a world with voices practically shouting at us, telling us how to raise our families. Co-sleeping versus crib sleeping. What you should be feeding them, how long to nurse them, babies in strollers versus wearing your babies. All the voices can be overwhelming.

Back when I had my first baby, Instagram wasn't even a thing yet, Facebook was picking up traction, and blogs were few and far between and not even on people's radars. Now, there are so many voices. And that's not even mentioning the actual people in our lives and their opinions.

We have all of these avenues we're willfully opening and letting into our lives. All these opinions, all these views on life, ideas, theories. Are they worth mimicking? Are these voices the "faithful and blameless" in the land? Or are they just the loudest?

> *"Do not let anyone who delights in false humility and the worship of angels disqualify you. Such a person also goes into great detail about what they have seen; they are puffed up with idle ideas by their unspiritual minds."*
>
> —Colossians 2:18 (NIV)

There are a lot of loud, idle ideas that have no biblical qualification whatsoever being thrown at us. Sometimes, these notions come from so-called Christians. We need to observe their lives and if what they are saying is actually backed up by what the Bible says. It's up to us to recognize the idle ideas that are trending and not give them the time of day. If everything the world is saying on how to do things is sounding sort of right to you, or if how you are mothering is starting to look very similar to how your unsaved neighbor is mothering her family, I'd be pretty sure you've been listening to the wrong voices in the land. You need to readjust the megaphones in your life.

Just because people have popular platforms that they can talk from doesn't mean they should be listened to—especially if these people (who call themselves Christians) have a bunch of celebrities endorsing them and telling you to read their books or listen to them. That should be a major red flag to us Christians. Remember, the Bible says that its message and people of Christ are like "the stench of death" to those who don't believe. The Bible says its message will bring discord and hate from those who don't believe in the saving name of Jesus. So if those who are not saved or who have no evidence of being saved are agreeing with the message of so-called Christians, my bet would be that those voices are not speaking biblical truth and should not be listened to. Psalm 16:3 (NLT) says, "The godly people in the land are my true heroes, I take pleasure in them." Who are we allowing to influence how we mother? Someone is.

Now that I've been in this mothering game for almost a decade, I could probably be considered one of those moms who has learned a thing or two. But you can still find me observing, I'm still seeking out wisdom, I'm still asking questions, and I'm still acquiring wisdom from those ahead of me. It's up to me who I'm listening to, who I'm surrounding myself with physically and mentally. Who am I allowing to speak into my life? Are those I'm listening to living a life I want to mimic?

WHO ARE WE LISTENING TO?

Back when I had three boys and I was pregnant with our fourth, we had my oldest sister and my brother-in-law and their family over for dinner. We were all hanging out around the dinner table talking, laughing, being together. Now my third born at the time was testing my husband and me as hard as he could. It was very normal for us to ask him to come to us and he'd look at us and run away. Or we would tell him no and he'd fall to the ground screaming. We would have to ask him multiple times to do even the smallest things. My husband and I had allowed this behavior to continue for so long that this was just normal to us. I can remember thinking, *We're going to have to get this kid into shape some time soon*; but for one reason or another, we had willingly turned a blind eye to the sin that was very apparent in our son's life.

That night, my brother-in-law did one of the most loving things he could do for us and his nephew. He very gently called us out on the behavior we were allowing with our son and how it wasn't biblical, how we hold our other sons to a higher standard, and how we need to call our youngest to that same standard.

Wham! Talk about a wake-up call!

We knew we weren't winning with this child, but it's almost like we needed a voice of someone we loved and respected telling us to reengage. And we did! When we aren't engaged in correcting our child's behavior, we really aren't that serious about trying to develop godly character in him at all. We can't leave our children to themselves and hope they turn out to love and mimic Jesus. Being left to themselves is the opposite of everything godly.

The voices we're seeking out or listening to matter a great deal. They matter because they help shape our families.

ACTION TIPS:

- Who are you seeking out to minister and speak into your life? In the flesh, I mean. No one? Find someone and learn. Make sure he or she is qualified to be speaking into your life. The qualities of godliness and compassion are a great place to start.
- What megaphones do you need to quiet down or cut off altogether in your life? Ask God to show you what voices He wants quieted so He has more freedom to speak to you.

14

ZERO-TOLERANCE POLICY

"Isn't it funny how day by day nothing changes, but when you look back, everything is different."

—C. S. Lewis

It was one of those days. That kind of day you wished you could just erase from your mothering history log. The day before this awful one, my husband and I had an argument. Not just the kind of little argument you deal with and hardly skip a beat. No, this was the kind of argument you hoped could get resolved sooner than the end of the week. But you had no expectations. Feelings were hurt, points weren't being made, and sides weren't being seen, heard, or understood. Feeling like you weren't sure you could ever like your spouse again—you know, those kinds of arguments.

The icing on the cake was that he left for a conference for the weekend before things got resolved. So my husband is gone and I'm left by myself with the kids. I'm left at home with unresolved hurts and some pretty raw emotions. Evening arrives and the boys are in bed. My baby at the time had been fighting a fever but seemed like he was on the mend. In reality, though, he was just waiting for nighttime to uncover all he had planned. Let's just put it this way: when dawn arrived that next morning and my toddler woke me before the sun had actually appeared, I still had a child's puke in my hair, piles of laundry covered in vomit, stains in the carpet still unattended to, and hours spent the night before trying to console an inconsolable baby. Only three hours of sleep under my belt and the undeniable desire to throw my hands up in the air and drop to the ground next to my toddler and throw a temper tantrum with him.

I remember looking at the clock and thinking, It's only 7:46 a.m.? How am I physically going to make it through this day? Moms can see clearly and quickly when a day is shaping up to be a rough one. We see the bad attitudes and the sin all over our toddler's face. We can hear the fussing and whining. Those days that started off the wrong way before morning appeared. We are exhausted already. We are dealing with our own emotions and feelings in that moment. One thing after another just keeps adding up to an awful day.

In those mornings, too often I have a tendency to very quickly raise my white flag of surrender. I can see that we are headed into a turbulent day and I want nothing to do with it. So I take great measures to try to avoid the day that God has set up for me. I want to pacify my fussy toddler and sort of forget about the zero-tolerance policy we strictly have in place toward fussing. Probably because in my heart, I'm fussing as much as he is. I don't want to focus on my kid's sin because it's just revealing my own.

Instead of dealing with sin head-on, I try to distract my kids or make excuses for their behavior: "He's so fussy because I'm almost sure he's still teething." Or I make excuses for my own behavior: "I barely got any sleep last night. I haven't had a conversation with an adult in days." I take on a "woe is me" attitude. I can start thinking about how hard my situation is with my kids. "It's just not fair. Don't I deserve a little bit of me time?" Instead of addressing these things that have risen up in my heart and the very evident sin of my children, I push them away and declare to the kids, "Today is a movie day!" I'm hoping to avoid any and all conflict that seems so close to the surface. I don't feel like disciplining and correcting wrong behavior today. (Remember how little sleep you got?) Engaging with my little people's character is so much work.

DO MORE THAN JUST SURVIVE

Sometimes we use the term "survival mode" to describe the day we are having. I've had plenty of those days. But I think I've had way more of those days than God wanted me to have. Are there legitimate days when we need to call an audible and or take a knee? Those days, we need to get everyone off the crazy cycle. So we switch up our day for the sake of morale. God absolutely gives us the freedom to have those days. But if we are mostly living in survival mode, I think we run the risk of missing out on the day and the growth that God set up for us. God wants us to do more than just survive motherhood. He's allowed you to be a mom, and He's given you these kids because He wants to use you to reach them. Is it wrong to hope and even pray for peaceful days or even long for them? No! I don't think so. But I have yet to experience real growth of my character and real, desperate closeness with my God only in the bright, cheery days.

Most of my growing pains have all taken place during the hard, never-ending, trying days. If I lean into my Savior and cry out for His strength to make it through the day, because my strength ran out a long time ago, then I get the chance to experience my Father answering my call for help. If I'm constantly avoiding these hard days, then I'm constantly forfeiting growth. Don't avoid those hard days; know that they have purpose.

I have a verse sitting on my desk. It says, "Establish the work of our hands for us—yes, establish the work of our hands" (Psalm 90:17, NIV). *I can love this verse, but I can also really struggle with it. I can take comfort in knowing that God has set up my day with the work He wants me to get done. But my struggle with this verse is when I don't like the looks of what He has for me. What if what He has for me that day are those little bad attitudes that drive me crazy? What if all He wants me to do is the next right thing, whether I feel like it or not? Which seems to be disciplining the sin of my children even while I'm sleep-deprived and feeling like all I'm doing is pouring myself out gaining nothing in return. If I'm doing the work the Lord has established for me that very minute or that hour or that day, then it's essential I do it. And that I do it well.*

A mom I follow on Instagram had the quote, "As a mom, you are mission-essential." Amen! You are essential in your children's lives. They need you to be always mission-minded; their souls could be depending on it.

> *"She was ambitious for 'higher and better things' but was enabled to learn that the person who would do great things well must practice daily on little ones, and she who would have the assistance of the Almighty in important acts, must be daily and hourly accustomed to consult His will in the minor affairs of life."*
>
> —Elisabeth Elliot

How often can I feel like my days are only full of "minor affairs"? He sees you, sister. He sees your heart. He sees your effort. He sees your steps of obedience out of faith. Don't believe the lie that what you do between your four walls of your home aren't seen. Whether it's a soft whimpering cry for help in the early morning hours while feeding that baby, knowing fully well this is the beginning of another hard day, or if it's silently pleading for help for the thousandth time in the middle of the night while cleaning up vomit from your child while your body and mind are literally aching for rest, He sees you. He has an eye on you and your character.

> *"You are as much serving God in looking after your own children, and training them up in God's fear, and minding the house, and making your household a church for God, as you would be if you had been called to lead an army to battle for the Lord of hosts."*
>
> —Charles Spurgeon

ACTION TIPS:

- On those hard days, don't raise your white flag of surrender too quickly! Stop and remember these are the days when growth can happen.
- Recognize your heart and feelings and attitude toward these days that wear on you. Could your reaction to these days be what God has His eye on changing in you?

15

FAITH LEADING

"Can we not count upon Him to give for us and each child just what we need if only we believe?"

—Andrew Murray

Faith. Everything I've talked about in this book has got to be done out of faith. It's faith in the Lord's sovereignty. Faith that He's in control. Faith that there will be a reward and a blessing and a harvest if we obey Him and follow His leading. If we position ourselves daily in front of our Father's throne to hear what He would have us do, we can confidently lead our own children—despite fears and weaknesses on our part. "Now faith is confidence in what we hope for and assurance about what we do not yet see" Hebrews 11:1 (NIV). We need to cling to faith and hope and believe that despite our sin and flaws, we will see a harvest in our children either in this world or the next.

We need to fight against doubts and feelings of inadequacy. It shouldn't matter what the world spits at us in rage because we won't conform to what they say is right. Our mothering should look different than most of the moms at the park (unless you're there with a play group from church). The way we parent should be different than how our neighbors parent because we're parenting according to how the Bible says to. But this all needs to be saturated with faith, bleeding out of every crack and crevice of our lives.

"Faith has never yet been disappointed."
—Andrew Murray

Isn't that one of the most valid statements you've ever read? Maybe you haven't experienced your faith being blessed because you've never stepped out with faith as a mother. Well, you still have time, so start now! Sometimes mothering out of faith can look scary and illogical and make you feel insecure, but I promise the moment you start, you'll find yourself securely in your Father's hands, being led by Him. He'll never lead you astray. I hope you believe that.

"Faith is the one condition through which the power and the salvation of God are given. Just believe. It is by faith that we throw ourselves and our children on Jesus and secure His blessing."
—Andrew Murray

If we only mother in the ways that feel easy and safe or within our comfort zone, then we miss out in mothering by faith. Sometimes, living a life of faith isn't always easy or comfortable.

Maybe you're prone to be fearful in your mothering. Andrew Murray also says, "Faith can banish fear!" But we can't continue mothering with fear leading us, hoping to live a faith-filled life. They can't coexist. I know my weaknesses and my sins can hinder my faith. I know that God is as big and mighty as I know Him to be. But can I really believe my kids are going to turn out okay despite my flaws and imperfections as a mom?

REGRETTABLY GUILTY

God is keenly aware of the areas we need to change in. He's aware of the sins we're prone to commit, the ones we absolutely hate but can't seem to get rid of—especially those areas that seem to come out so loudly only in front of our children. Have you ever gotten to the end of the day, and you're lying in bed at night with tears in your eyes thinking about how you treated your kids that day? Do the mean words you said to your child out of anger keep replaying over and over in your head? Then, you get up and walk into their room just so you can look at them sleeping peacefully and think, *I am a terrible mother. How could I ever treat this child of mine like that?* You agonize with guilt and regret. You're almost certain you've already messed up your kids with your mistakes as a parent. You fear that you're going to pass your weaknesses and tendencies to your children.

If you can relate at all to me, or if you have also made those late-night guilt trips into your child's room, then let me offer you some encouragement from one sinful mom to another. Remember that we are all sinful humans who have all been given little sinful humans to raise. God doesn't expect us to be perfect. In fact, He *knows* it's impossible for us to be perfect. Thankfully, perfection isn't a standard that needs to be met to be a godly mother. He has already forgiven our mess-ups today, yesterday, and tomorrow. And in His sovereignty, He deemed it best to make you—out of every woman in the world—the mom to your kids, flaws and all. Our sins don't surprise our Heavenly Father. He knows all about them, and yet He still chose you to be the mom to your little ones. We have to trust that God knows what He's doing and is sovereign over all.

Have you ever thought about the fact that the very sin that plagues you can actually be used as a powerful testimony in your life for your children to see? That this sin can be a picture of God's all-powerful ability to change lives? We can be a living, breathing picture of hope to our children. A hope of a changed life.

Obviously, our goal and desire is to live free of sin. I'm not making an excuse or making light of the consequences that everyone's sin has on those closest to us. But we are going to mess up in front of our kids. We are going to sin against them. Let us be the prime example of humbly seeking forgiveness from our children. Honestly and humbly communicate with them that Mom is trying to obey Jesus just like they are being taught.

LOUD, UGLY SINS

I have a tendency to get angry and lose my temper toward my sons. My natural emotion that I resort to—whether it's because of frustration, hurt, sadness, or stress—is anger. My tendency is to yell and bark when my children aren't acting how I want them to be acting. I hate this about me. I hate how it hurts my kids. I hate how it causes them to tear up. I hate how, when I'm sinning in this area, I'm giving them an inaccurate picture of how the Lord treats us.

So, what do I do about this loud, ugly sin of mine? I can live a life full of regret and guilt for the things I've done, being hard on myself and becoming my worst critic, which often leads to self-pity and inaccurate views of myself. If I'm living this way, it's showing my kids how *not* to accept the grace and forgiveness that Jesus so preciously bought for me. Or I learn to draw often, freely and gratefully, from the grace that's available to me. I can also live my life riddled with fear of how my weaknesses are going to affect my children, which is a lack of trust in the Lord's sovereignty. Living by fear is saying to God, "My sin is too big for you to handle." He's big enough! He can handle your sin. He already did! Leave your sin at the foot of the cross where it belongs.

"'What hour I am afraid I will trust in thee'; such words have a thousand times over been the stay of the trembling but trusting handmaid of the Lord." —Andrew Murray

We need to trust our Heavenly Father. Instead of living by fear, we need to call out to Him for His help and to believe His promises. We can put our sins and mess-ups where they rightfully belong: at the foot of the cross. Then, we do our part and we keep working on saying no to our sin. We keep begging for the Lord's help to change us in these areas. But when I fail by yelling at one of my kids, I repent to the Lord and thank Him for already forgiving this sin of mine. Then, I go to that child and get on his eye level, cup his face in my hands, and ask for his forgiveness. I tell that child, "That's not how the Lord wants me to treat you. Jesus never treats us that way, and I shouldn't treat you that way." Sometimes we talk more about it, but other times, it's that quick. We hug. We move on.

My kids know that Mom isn't perfect. They hear me praying for myself during the day or at mealtimes. They hear me when I acknowledge when I mess up. I don't want my kids growing up thinking that my sins are okay because I never acknowledged them or called them what they were—sins. How confusing could that be for our kids?

When we sin against our kids, they feel it. They feel that it was wrong. We need to acknowledge and admit when we're wrong and ask for forgiveness. I'm hoping that when my boys are older, they can say something like, "Mom used to get angry and yell, but she doesn't anymore. God clearly changed her." I'm hoping to be a first-hand picture to my children of a person changed by God. A person who had grips of sin in her life but has broken free from them—thanks to her Heavenly Father.

"Step by step, amidst many a failure, the honest effort to do God's will cannot remain without its reward." —Andrew Murray

ACTION TIPS:

- Acknowledge the loud, ugly sins in your life. (And the quiet ones those can be just as deadly.)
- Search Scripture for promises and commands regarding these areas.
- Through prayer, plead with the Lord to change and grow you.
- When you mess up, because you will, practice humility before your children and ask for their forgiveness. Especially if you sinned against them. Even if they aren't old enough to verbally respond back to you, get in the habit of asking for forgiveness and communicating the powerful and life-changing message that our Father offers us grace and forgiveness daily! Live in that message and invite your children to live there too.

AFTERWORD

"Only one life 'twill soon be past,
only what's done for Christ will last."

—C. T. Studd

As I bring this to a close, my hope and my countless prayers over these writings is that something you read here encouraged you and resonated with you. My hope is that you feel spurred on to keep learning and growing in your role as a godly mom. Maybe you were challenged or convicted by something that was said. Know this: what I wrote here is just one mom's story about what God has taught her in her first eight years of motherhood.

I tried to be careful not to just write my opinions and biases toward mothering. I tried my hardest to recall all that I could consciously remember that the Lord has taught me through the sleep-deprived years with babies and toddlers. Ultimately, my goal here was to point all eyes that read this book to the One who is the perfect parent. As a flawed child of God who is in desperate need of His mercies and grace (hourly!), I needed to testify of all the things

He has done for me. I needed to give Him all the glory He so richly deserves. It's been a burning in my heart for a while now and I had to write it down.

You've just read my stories of how He has come through for me time and time again, and I want to remind you He wants to do the same for you. You just read what He has slowly, over the last eight years, been laying on my heart and teaching me. It's what He has been teaching me Monday through Sunday. Through all the ordinary days with seemingly little happening. He's been working. As I've been writing down these stories, lessons, and thoughts, I've been pleading with the Lord that these wouldn't give a false, glorified picture of the flawed people we are. I tried to be as honest as possible with my struggles as a mom and with the struggles of my children.

My husband and I by no means have arrived or have it all figured out. We are still working through big things with our kids and we know we aren't even close to being done. We are working every day to hang on to their hearts. We are still making choices as parents based only on faith alone, not knowing the outcome yet, hoping these choices will result in a godly harvest. I don't have this mothering thing figured out. I still have big things that I need to change. Big, evident areas of sin that I need to win in. But I'm relying more heavily on my Heavenly Father than ever before, and I think that's something. It spurs me on.

When I started writing this book, I knew from the beginning I wanted to add some of my favorite and most convicting quotes from authors of old. I quoted Elisabeth Elliot and J. C. Ryle often because they are my spirit animals and I can't wait to meet them in eternity. Everything they wrote should be read. You won't regret it. Most of the poems I quoted were either Amy Carmichael's or Amy's favorite poems. She's also one of my favorites and is on my top list of people to look for first when I get to Heaven. Andrew Murray and Oswald Chambers made it into my writings because these men don't mince words. They spoke boldly and were full of conviction. I have yet to regret reading their books, although it takes ten times longer to read their stuff because they're heavy and wordy; but their words cut deep and I keep coming back for more. I challenge you to read these authors' books.

Do me a favor and go read these heroes and heroines of the faith. They are linguistic champions, they were full of wisdom and discernment, and they had long lives marked by faith. Their stories will bless you, I'm sure of it.

So, fellow moms, fellow sisters on the frontlines of the battlefield, fellow daughters of the King: rise to the challenge of living a life that looks differently than the other families' lives on your street. Rise to the challenge of hearing God's leading and saying yes to Him and following Him. Rise to the challenge of saying no to the world we live in and how it says we should be raising our babies.

Answer God's calling to you to mother *His* way. Be brave and bold. If you are tired and weary, take a new, firm grip knowing you are not alone. Not even close. If you are knee-deep in babies, diapers, and toddlers with dark rings around your eyes that you're sure won't ever go away, if you think you'll never sleep through the night uninterrupted again, if you feel like you're failing through these tiring yet critical years, just remember: You. Are. Not. Alone. He sees you. He wants to help you through these years that He has laid before you. Grip tight to His hand and allow yourself to be led. He's not going to lead you astray or leave you hanging.

We can do more than just survive these years. We can live these years with confidence and strength because we are following our Lord and relying on Him alone.

I'm going to finish this book with a poem that I cherish. Every time I read it, I get goosebumps. I read this poem for the first time after I was about three-fourths through writing this book, and when I read it, I was dumbfounded.

So here is the poem I read that's directly in line with my heart's desire and my hope behind my written words.

Call Back

"If you have gone a little way ahead of me, call back;
'Twill cheer my heart and help my feet along the stony track;
And if, perchance, Faith's light is dim, because the oil is low,
Your call will guide my lagging course as wearily I go.
Call back, and tell me that He went with you into the storm;
Call back, and say He kept you when the forest's roots were torn;
That when the heavens thundered and the earthquake shook the hill,
He bore you up and held you where the very air was still.
O friend, call back and tell me, for I cannot see your face;
They say it glows with triumph, and your feet bound in the race;
But there are mists between us, and my spirit eyes are dim,
And I cannot see the glory, though I long for word of Him.
But if you'll say He heard you when your prayer was but a cry,
And if you'll say He saw you through the night's sin-darkened sky,
If you have gone a little way ahead, O friend, call back,
'Twill cheer my heart and help my feet along the stony track."

—Author Unknown

ACKNOWLEDGMENTS

There are a couple of people I have to acknowledge by name. Without these people, this little book you're holding in your hands would not be a reality.

First, Joy Hill. This woman! It was her idea that maybe what I had on my heart could be a book. She was the voice saying to me, "Hannah, write it down!" Your encouragement literally gave me the confidence to try. Thank you for being my sounding board and a steady voice of truth to me. Thank you, dear cousin.

Then there is Shayla. You were far beyond just my editor. Thank you for your wisdom and guidance and mad skills when it came to writing and all things publishing. You were literally an answer to my prayers. I could not have done this without you. Thank you.

Next, my own mom. Mom, you are the real MVP here. My living, breathing, in-the-flesh example of a woman who laid down her life daily for her seven kids and still does to this day. Your voice and words of truth throughout my life have influenced how I live, how I speak, and how I mother my own kids. Thank you, Mom, for showing me that a woman who allows the Lord to lead her in her mothering can change and influence lives. You have seven lives that are proof of that and are eternally grateful for your sacrifice.

Then there's Shane. My favorite person on this round planet. Thank you, baby, for helping this dream of mine come to be. Thank you for holding down the fort and letting me escape to go write when you could see that crazy look in my eye and know I had to go get it off my chest and mind. Thank you for all those nights of being okay with the fact that I would bring my laptop to bed, knowing you were going to be falling asleep to the sound of typing. Thank you for being a willing ear when I was working on a chapter and had to talk it out loud to someone. Thank you for being my leader, my protector, my favorite person to dream with. Being your wife and being a parent with you is truly beyond what I deserve, and the honor is all mine. Love you.

To my sons, my mighty men. I am so proud of the men you boys are growing into. You are my heartbeat, my greatest joy, and my favorite calling. Thank you for letting me tell (well, you didn't really have a choice) all our stories so far. Remember, we tell our stories to bring glory and honor to our King! It's not about us; it's always about Him. I love doing life with you, boys. I truly and deeply love being your mom.

"Such men don't grow on every bush."
—Author Unknown

ABOUT THE AUTHOR

Hannah Unger has been heavily involved in mothering since her first son was born. Since then, three more sons have come along just to ensure she stays outnumbered by a healthy margin. She and her husband of twelve years live in Lincoln, Nebraska, also known as God's country. They are trying their best to wrangle their stallion sons and raise them according to biblical standards. Hannah has the honor of speaking and encouraging other mothers in church meetings, seminars, moms' groups, face-to-face, and through her Instagram account. She is the author of *White-Knuckled Mothering*.

Connect with the Author

Instagram.com/hannahfaithunger

LEAVE A REVIEW

If you enjoyed White-Knuckled Mothering, will you please consider writing a review on Amazon and Goodreads? Reviews help self-published authors make their books more visible to new readers.

Goodreads:
www.goodreads.com/book/show/44604574-white-knuckled-mothering

Amazon:
www.amazon.com/dp/B07PYN4CTK

NOTES

1. AUTHORITY: IS IT REALLY NECESSARY?

1. J. C. Ryle, *The Duties of Parents: Parenting Your Children God's Way* (ANEKO Press, 2018).
2. Ibid.
3. Ibid.

10. SLOW SOWING YEARS

1. Elisabeth, Elliot, *The Shaping of a Christian Family: How My Parents Nurtured My Faith* (Revell, 2005).
2. Ibid.

Made in the USA
Middletown, DE
15 April 2019